Wild and Wise Women Around the World

Ten Inspiring Women share their Feminine Fire

Beverly Adamo

Published by Wild and Wise® Women Enterprises, Inc
March, 2019
ISBN: 9781733811804

Editor: Danielle Anderson
Typeset: Greg Salisbury
Book Cover Design: Judith Mazari

Dedication

To ALL of the Wild and Wise® Women Around the World, you ARE the change that is needed to heal this world.

From Bev Adamo: to my extraordinary daughter, Chiara, my courageous mom JoAn, and to the awesome Wild and Wise® authors around the world who answered the call, found their courage, bared their souls, and shared their stories to inspire and empower other women.

From Holly Chadwick: to my mom for her inspiring courage, and to my husband James, my soulmate and unwavering support.

From Jane Beausire: to the magnificent female warrior in all of us, and with special love and gratitude to Papatuanuku, the mother of us all.

From Juanita Figueroa: to my AMAZING and patient husband Manuel, my children, and my mother Becky. To all those that were part of my amazing journey thus far.

From Karen McGinty: with Love to Stephen, for always loving and supporting me unconditionally and without limits.

From Lia Venet: to my first and biggest teacher, my mother, and my father, who has softened and opened with age, in appreciation for loving me no matter how uncomfortable my strong character made them feel. To my soulmate and love of my life, Philippe, in gratitude for the growth of our deep love over these last twenty-five years of marriage. To my old soul children, Téva and Ange-Elise, who have become my teachers.

From Nina Luchka: to my incredible children Aspen, Cruz, Knox and Steihl. Your beautiful, unique personalities have made me understand motherhood and be the best person I can be. To my husband, Vince, who constantly encourages me to go for my dreams, whatever they are. To all the moms who think they are alone in their struggles and daily challenges, don't lose yourself. I send my love to all of you.

From Stephanie Roman: to Emily Rose, my life-changing life coach, and to my mom Ida Noack for showing me what a real Badass woman looks like.

From Sue Bonzell: to my mom and my dad who paved the way to who I am now, and to my life coach Jen Julius who helped me get out of my own way!

From Terry Jackson: to Lee, my husband and soulmate, and to Kim and Wendy, my daughters and best friends. I am so grateful for my mentor and the teachers who helped me grow, and for the little girl inside of me who will never give up.

From Wanda King: to my amazing, supportive and loving family—Chip, Desiree, Harper, and Justin. They never stopped believing in me and supported me in my vision to make a positive difference in the world.

Testimonials

"A MUST READ for every woman – and every girl becoming a woman – around the world.

Wild and Wise Women Around the World is like the most delicious buffet that you can continue to nibble on over and over again. Taking big bites or small, each one is filled with truth, raw emotion, authenticity, humor, sadness, joy and so much more.

In today's world, this book is a triumph. I encourage you to have many copies on hand, I know I will. This book is my go-to gift – perfect for grandmothers and mothers, daughters and granddaughters, sisters and soul-sisters – reminding every wild and wise woman in our lives of two key takeaways from these pages. You are not alone, and you are loved.

I do believe we can all use more of that, and this book delivers it. "

**Christa Thompson, Founder of Wild and Wise® Women
CEO of Christa Rayne Consulting**

"I loved meeting these ten women –– getting to know their lives, loves, tragedies and triumphs. They remind me that our community is powerful and we are stronger together than we are apart. This is a beautiful and heartfelt celebration of women who ARE wild and wise!"

Susan Rook D'Ettorre - fmr. CNN Anchor/Host TalkBack Live

Acknowledgements

Expressing appreciation is a key part of being and living as a Wild and Wise® Woman. We trust that along the way, we have shared our gratitude with those who have made this book a reality. If in reading this you know that you contributed to the manifestation of this book and do not see your name listed below, please add it. Yes, really!

Thank you to Christa Thompson, founder of Wild and Wise® Women and Wild and Wise® Sisterhood, for your vision, your dedication, your love for all Wild and Wise®.

Thank you to Kristen Cook, Courtney Dayon, Rubina Justa, and Ashmeeta Mehendiratta, Team Awesome at Wild and Wise®, for your extraordinary support along this path.

Thank you to Julie Salisbury, founder of Influence Publishing, and her amazing Team Awesome for the technical expertise and magical structure around which this book has come into being.

Thank you to the inspiring authors in this book for finding the courage to share their stories, and to their family and friends for providing the awesome support that is needed in a collaboration such as this.

Finally, thank you to the Divine for leading me into envisioning this book and guiding other women to find their voices and share their stories in order to inspire and empower others.

Contents

Introduction

November 1, 2018. Who knew that this day was the US National Authors' Day? I certainly did not when I put the call out to invite women from the Wild and Wise® Women Community to join me in an unprecedented collaborative book series. The Universe, however, had a grand and Divine plan to bring together ten extraordinary women literally from around the world to tell their stories of impactful experiences in their lives and how their Feminine Fire inspired and led them to phenomenal and transformational choices in and around those life circumstances.

Wild and Wise® Women (W3) was purposefully created with a big mission: to provide a space where all my soul sisters could gather and know that they are powerful force. The message to these women is, "You are a badass. A superstar. A creative genius. You are the glue that holds your family, your company, and your community together, selflessly giving every ounce of your being to everyone around you." But darling, we were never meant to sacrifice all that we are. We are Change Agents, Creators, and Givers of Life, and it's time to reclaim who you really are.

This is why the Sacred Space of W3 was created. We need a space to stop thinking, stop doing, and just be; a space where we reclaim our Wild and our Wise and truly get to know ourselves. W3 is committed to providing everything you need—the steps, support, solidarity, and strength—to design the highest, most passion-filled, most success-full vision for YOUR life without sacrificing your dreams, your sanity, or your overall well-being along the way.

So today, I invite you to slow down and just breathe. At W3

and in this book, the well is deep and the inspiration flows. You are free to be exactly who you are, and I promise you this: when you join hands with this sisterhood of nearly 300,000 wild and wise women, you will never be alone again. W3 is with you, holding the roadmap and cheering you on from the passenger's seat through every leg of your incredible journey!

However, W3 was only the beginning. From that space, the Wild and Wise® Sisterhood was born. The Wild and Wise® Sisterhood believes that empowered women empower other women through the Wild and Wise® Butterfly Effect. Sisterhood is about supporting one another to live our best lives and celebrating the brilliance that each of us brings to the table.

The Sisterhood is a membership, and each woman empowers her sisters as we all walk this journey together, refusing to play small in our lives. The Sisterhood empowers women we may never meet—women artisans from across the globe who have crafted items for membership gift boxes and share their love with the Sisterhood by sharing their handmade crafts with us. We reinvest a HUGE portion of gross revenue back into the artisan communities we partner with, and the Wild and Wise® Projects funded by the membership boxes and other products and services transform even more lives through supporting initiatives that improve health care, education, work conditions, and so much more.

This book is one of the products that will continue to extend the reach of the Wild and Wise® Butterfly Effect, as the royalties from your purchase will go directly to one of these transformational projects. Know that YOUR contribution through the purchase of this book will be supporting the improvement of the quality of life to women around the world!

When I issued the invitation for ten women to find and

share their voice, their vision, and their victories with the world, the intention was set to attract, by Divine Appointment, the perfect sacred circle of ten women who together would be the magical combination of diverse and yet cohesive messages that the world needs most right now. The Universe certainly delivered, and I am in awe of the Wild and Wise® Women who answered that call and kept their Divine Appointment with their destiny to impact the world.

I am honored to introduce these amazing authors to you in this collaborative and catalytic collection of stories as these women brave their own demons and bring their unique and fascinating voices to the world. I have absolute faith that these stories, these victories, will inspire women around the world to take on the challenges that might otherwise daunt the most courageous souls on the planet. I can also guarantee that these ten authors have transformed, expanded, and inspired themselves and each other during this magical and miraculous journey of bringing their Feminine Fire to the world!

You, Divine Reader, are invited to read every word and waste nary a drop of the Wild and Wise® stories contained herein. The Universe is calling you to be visible, and you can start by "seeing" these ten women as they honor themselves by allowing their authentic selves to be seen and heard. You will come to know, as I have, that all of these women are brilliant, intuitive, worthy, holy, wholly unique, admired, and beloved Women of Spirit and all beings. They are, in fact, YOU! Enjoy, Divine Reader, knowing that as these stories inspire and activate your essence, you too will be living and sharing YOUR Feminine Fire. And in doing so, you join the Sisterhood of Wild and Wise® Women, finding your passion, being of service in the world, and creating the extraordinary life you are destined to live.

Foreword

I have to say that seeing the Wild and Wise Women Around the World collaboration come to life has been an experience of such honour, pride and love that I know in the process I have become a raving fan of every single author on these pages, and even more importantly, of the millions of women that these stories represent.

Words are so powerful; and messengers are so incredibly vital as they contribute to the richness of our lives and personal experiences. We are in an incredible time in history where it is not only healing, it is not only sacred, it is not only courageous, and it is not only more significant than ever ... it is a responsibility that our voices are heard and our stories shared. Why? Because your voice, your story, your message, your experience ... matter.

Not just the authors on these pages, that is what is so magical about it. The voice and story of every one of us across the globe shapes not only our own experience, but each other's. And it is the light of our stories that banish darkness and remind us that we are not alone.

Honestly, it's bigger than this book. The Wild and Wise movement began in 2010, not so long ago, and whether you know it or not - it's a tribe that you already belong to. It's a family that already loves you. It's a safe space and safe place that you can call home. And this book is another call ... a call in the wild ... echoing through the trees and bouncing off the mountains. It's a call to you.

So I invite you to settle in. Open your heart to real voices of real wild and wise women who have come together by divine appointment, and in doing so - I know - are contributing to healing the world.

Yes, healing the world. Sound lofty? It's not. Words, stories, community, truth and love heal the world - bit by bit, page by page, story by story, word by word.

So again, settle in and join us. Join these women, who are just like you and I, who are filled with feminine fire, who are running with wolves, who are living wild and wise. Join us as they share their own transformations with you so that you too can transform.

And then in true wild and wise fashion I invite you to share as well. Share this book with the wild and wise women in your life, heck read it together - in community - write notes in the margins, underline passages that move you, use post-its for pages you want to come back to, uncover the depths of the women in your circle through this book. That's the truest gift of all.

And here's what I am 100% sure of. You too have a story to tell and a message to share. You too have words inside of you that aching to come out that, purely with their release into the light, will change the world for the better. You ARE a wild and wise woman and the world needs you.

So be brave. Today, tomorrow, next week, next year ... and start by reaching out to the brave and passionate leader of the Wild and Wise tribe, Bev Adamo and let her help you ... release your story.

It is my immense honour to introduce you to Wild and Wise Women Around the World. Use it well, and always remember ... You Are Loved xo.

Christa
Founder of Wild and Wise Women

About Bev Adamo

As owner and CEO of Wild and Wise® Enterprises, Inc, Bev's purpose on this planet is to lead herself and other powerful, awesome, and amazing women into the truth of who we are. She is a huge believer in self-love, witnessing her own healing as well as the healing of those around her. She has experienced the miracle of life, death, and rebirth through the unique and inspiring experience of her husband Ric dying in her arms and then fighting his way back to life for Three Reasons. As she walked through the internal and external hardships of life, she was able to gain a bird's eye view on why we suffer and how to transform our suffering into healing and joy.

Bev is a Certified Dream Coach®, One Page Business Plan® consultant, Simple Spiritual Energy practitioner, program facilitator, inspirational speaker, and licensed True Purpose™ coach. She is also the author of *Catch Your Star*, The *Three Reasons*, and soon to be released, *The Fourth Reason*. Everything that she does is inspired by her personal experiences and by working with people from all walks of life. Her aim as a Doctor of Divinity and an ordained minister is to awaken the souls to the truth of their unique brilliance.

Bev Adamo
Owner and CEO
Wild and Wise Women Enterprises, Inc
793 Tracy Blvd. #359
Tracy, CA 95376
bev@wildandwisewomen.com

1

Playing with the Darkness

by Karen McGinty

Playing with the Darkness

Growing up in Lancashire, England, I had no idea that women were born to be empowered; men were definitely "in charge," and although I observed women being vocal and controlling, I never saw the true strength that comes from a quiet place. Love felt conditional and withheld if you dared to scream out, whilst anger was NEVER allowed—heavens above, what would people think!

It was a time when the only way to survive was to be a very good girl who was seen but not heard. Being labelled as "over-sensitive" or "not like everybody else" was the worst insult of all; I didn't even realize at the time that my voice was being sealed. As a result, I grew to hold on to and hide away any emotion that was considered negative.

This was also a time when the #MeToo movement was beyond the reach of the clouds and it seemed safer to be compliant and stay silent. A time when you didn't even realize that the man who patted your bottom and lingered a little too long was not only wrong and stealing your innocence but was also stealing your voice. A time when the head teacher who "teasingly" trapped you to slide his hand under your skirt and between your thighs in a "tickling way," forcing you to stay still until you managed to control your squeals, was not only abusing his power but also teaching you it was safer to stay quiet. These men knew they could win, because who would I tell? I assumed my "giddiness" was to blame for bringing attention to myself by being both seen AND heard.

Shame dined well during the first thirty years of my life.

And yet, apart from a few unsavory individuals, the Big People who I grew up around only acted the way they did because they, too, were victims of the social conditioning of their own generation and seemed unaware that they were blindly squashing my spirit in many ways. I only had to listen to my mum talk about her life growing up to realize that elements of it were very harsh. I know that whilst navigating her own emotional baggage, she brought me up the very best way she knew how and taught me by example what it is to have a joy in nature. It is also to my mum that I can credit all the kindness I possess.

Despite what I've been describing so far, I did have a lovely childhood. Although things sometimes happened that I did not like which were creating patterns of behavior for my future life, I was not consciously aware of them and knew no different.

One benefit of a 1970s childhood was that I had oodles of free time alone in nature. I remember the joy of streams and trees and tadpoles and flowers. Mother Nature has always been around me, loving me like she does and connecting me to her heart.

My most poignant memories of people always come alongside an association with the earth. Anytime I smell a redcurrant bush or see white daisies, I am instantly reminded of my dad and can picture him next to the garage in our first house. Whenever I am in a deliciously intoxicating pine forest, my mum appears in my mind, and I remember the early evening picnic where her face shone as she whispered for me to look out for fairies. The grass in summer always reminds me of my beautiful baby brother, and I can picture the time when we lay in the shade during the heatwave of '76 and I taught him how to say my name.

My own personal joy, one that belonged solely to me, was a very secret space where most of the fairies lived; it was a sun-dappled glen next to a hidden stream, and in the spring it would be carpeted with bluebells and speckled with buttercups.

I can still feel the bliss of yesterday when I sink into that place, remembering the feel of the earth as my toes danced and wiggled against the delightfully-scented magic.

Looking back, I realize my Big People also had a deep connection to nature, without possibly even realizing it, and the Love within them left them willing and eager to share their precious free time with all of us together. If I close my eyes I can hear the rumbling laughter of family happiness and feel the warmth of the stones we would heat in the campfire to sit on, keeping us toasty in the evening air. There was often more than a dozen of us going on endless weekend trips for picnics at the beach or beside streams in meadows. There was always lots of food and singing—the latter usually followed after the men had returned from the pub and the women had finished clearing away the dishes, in a time when no-one thought to question the inequality. But still, the joy and noise of people letting go of their everyday worries made for a fun place to be. There was joy in the abandon.

My favorite memory is even more precious because it was a time when my dad and I were the only two people awake on earth—or so he told me. We were driving down to Cornwall for our summer holiday, and I had the very special privilege of being allowed to sleep in the front seat. I remember waking with my legs resting on dad's lap, and as the sun rose through the dawn clouds an early morning fog swirled low from the fields and edged onto the road. Dad whispered that it was fairy mist and we were so lucky to see it, because only the people who were the first awake in the world could *sometimes* catch a glimpse. I have since seen rolling mist many times in life, but I have never again seen it literally dance as it did during this magical moment.

These early childhood memories would rescue me during

many a challenging time that was to come. I have always had the ability to sink into simple wildness, where Love is deep and all encompassing. Mother Earth's energy connects me to all that is God-like and Divine, whilst the wonder and joy that I feel when I'm surrounded by nature helps me to expand into my Truth.

People still often passed judgement and the "what are you like" brigade never stopped marching, but I was lucky always to be able to cling to the Earth and the Heavens in a beautiful (and often secret) dance.

As the 1970s slowly tightened its trousers and the patriarchy wound into the 1980s, the collective fear of being different seemed to grip even more suppressively to the ether. The establishment clung to control, the media judged hatefully, and some authority figures appear to have abused even deeper and colluded together to hide their secrets to the extent that they have only just come to light today.

I now know I am an empath and my "over-sensitivity" is a gift, but back then I was intuitively feeling the emotional state of another person *without* the ability to understand what was happening. Lacking the awareness of how NOT to absorb the energy and pain around me, the stress of it all was beginning to take its toll and my natural light began to grow heavy. I had learned to be extremely good at people-pleasing, and my standard response to everyone about everything was to say I was sorry, even though in retrospect I was apologizing for nothing more than breathing.

Whilst I was still compliantly smiling on the surface, the anger and hurt was building and beginning to eat away at me, although I didn't recognize it at the time. My over-loaded cells were trying their best to hold on to all the feelings I swallowed, but eventually their barriers broke and the dam burst…

In 2001, I was diagnosed with cancer. While there were many facets to my healing journey, the final part of my "Karen has cancer" story took place over seven days and seven VERY LONG nights that would change my perspective on the world and allow me for the first time in my life to truly step into my own Power.

We had been having an unusually hot October and I was tiring from six months of chemotherapy, so I went to bed for an afternoon rest. I remember that my chest was feeling tight at the time, and I later discovered that I stopped breathing shortly after falling asleep. The next thing I was aware of was "lifting" out of my body and floating upwards through a rainbow. My human-ness was left behind as I continued rising until I felt lighter and surrounded by more Love that I can convey in human words. It was like a thousand orgasms and then some—apologies to God if I am ruining Creation with my clumsy words—but it was bliss upon bliss and knowing upon knowing. I was connected to all and instantly aware of everyone and everything, both separately and together. I had the deep knowing that through everyone's pain on earth, all was perfectly orchestrated and as it was meant to be. This was all and this was it; the mystery belonged to me, and I had the key.

I wanted to stay here, even though I had Connor, my most precious three-year-old boy, back on earth. My maternal instinct was to protect and be with him at all cost, but surprisingly the feeling of omnipresence was so strong that I felt Connor was also a part of it. I knew that although he would feel great pain if I left the earth, the bigger picture meant that he would one day also experience and understand the Love and the reason for everything.

My dad then appeared to me, smiling. At this point it

had been thirteen years since he died, so I fell into his arms, overjoyed to be held by him. After what seemed like hours and equally like no time at all, he whispered that it was time for me to go back. I remember wanting to stay—*not* because of him, but because of this feeling of all-encompassing Love.

He spoke kindly. "You need to go back for Connor. This isn't your time."

I knew I had a choice and that I could remain here if I wanted, but I also felt he was right and nodded reluctantly. He smiled again, and then I felt my body become heavy as I started to sink back through the rainbow and landed with a thud. I woke up on my knees, gasping for breath and life.

I was in awe and felt that it had been a complete privilege to have been allowed a tiny peep beyond the veil. And yet, how quickly my human side was to forget what I'd been shown!

After the "Rainbow Dream," I immediately began to get frustrated. My tumors continued to grow at an alarming rate, and I couldn't understand why I wasn't getting better. I'd spent the past few months visualizing myself well, learning to understand the emotional cause of my illness, and clearing the un-expressed emotions I'd held inside. I had been healing in nature every day and releasing and forgiving the past. At times, I'd explode in fury as I felt and processed a lifetime of frustration and pent-up anger; then, I'd physically heave as frozen fear began to dislodge and wriggle to the surface, wanting to be looked at and cleared. After all this work, my ego believed that because I had taken my healing in hand and faced my fear of dying, I would now completely heal.

The rainbow dream had been trying to tell me something, but I hadn't been ready to listen. So, I was now about to get another lesson in trusting and fully letting go.

The next night, my first panic attack brutally awoke me

with its severity. It seemed to come from nowhere. I had no concept I was panicking, feeling only the nearness of death. The heavy gloom and gripping terror clutched at my chest as I felt control slip from my grasp. Before having Connor, I'd worked as a nurse and had witnessed many a panicking patient. I had always been gentle towards them as I calmly encouraged them to normalize their breathing, but I'm sad to say that I never fully understood the terror and helplessness they were feeling. Until now.

These panic attacks continued on and off for an entire week, the longest episode lasting non-stop for five hours. One even caught me by surprise as I was driving on a busy motorway; how I managed to control myself until the next service station and keep "surface calm" for Connor, I can only attribute to some higher force.

Due to a promotion at work, we had relocated to a different part of the country only a few weeks prior to my becoming ill, and so I had no family close to help and no friends in the area at the time. Universal timing meant that my husband, Stephen, was working away from home at the time these attacks surfaced, and Kim, my spiritual teacher and go-to place of comfort and clarity, was unreachable that week. It seems I have always had to be alone to face my trials of fear and learn to dance with my darkness unaccompanied.

Floundering with fear and desperately in drama, I reverted to a medical explanation and decided the cancer must have spread to my lungs. I headed to the hospital, petrified, and was immediately admitted for an emergency scan.

I had always craved reassurance from hospital staff but never got enough to assuage my fears. I do understand in this day and age of litigation why the medical profession is so factual and always have to give both ends of the scale, even though the best-case scenario always sounded like a death sentence to me. However, on this occasion, the caring but pragmatic head-nurse who had been with me since my diagnosis gently squeezed my shoulder, looked into my eyes, and affirmed, "It *will* be all right, Karen." THAT was what I needed to hear. To any doctors out there who are reading this, it is NOT false hope to be blindly optimistic. It is manifesting possibility, and it is co-creating and healing dis-ease.

As soon as the head-nurse uttered those words, I had a "eureka" moment. The part of my soul which knew eternity urged the human part of me that wanted to control my healing to let go of fear and drama and trust the flow of the Universe—to feel any residual emotional pain, and to trust that I would fall into Love. Paradoxically, I was still engrained with the need for the tangible, 3D results, and although they ran the test through as an emergency I still had to wait a long, tight-chested twenty-four hours to hear them.

I often have spirit guides and can always feel Angels around me, but this night seemed to be an initiation and I could not sense a single being, apart from one silent and very stern looking Chinese man. I was being invited to trust Love and have faith that Connor would also be safe *regardless* of whether I lived or died, and it took literally everything I had to gracefully surrender to the thought of potentially leaving my most precious baby to the care of others. I had to know all was well. I had to trust that the Universe had my and Connor's highest good in hand and let go of my human need to control.

When I woke up the next day, even though the need for huge gulps of air continued, everything literally dazzled. The leaves on the trees sparkled, and I was in awe and bliss with the Light and the Life and the Love.

The phone call from the hospital came. "Karen, good news,

it hasn't spread. Nothing has shrunk, but nothing has grown bigger either." Even though I was being told I still had cancer, my joy was immense.

It was only a short while later that I realized my panicked breathing had stopped at the exact moment of my relief. I learned then how powerful I was, and everything I had been learning about mind and body connected. If I believed I was well and moved my head out of the way so my heart could take over and guide me, then I would heal.

Unfortunately, it took more than this one event for me to learn this lesson. A by-product of having been ill was that for several years afterwards, if I ever dropped into fear I found myself convinced I was dying. I would suddenly have a head/back/tummy ache, and after focusing on it and consciously feeling it grow, I would become adamant that I was going to die in a much more painful way than "just" cancer. This would be a big, dramatic death.

The first few times this happened, I would take myself seriously and go ashen-faced to the doctor, even though I'd be in part kicking myself for giving away my new-found power and knowing. The doctor would always err on the side of caution and send me for further testing. Each time a result came back—always negative—the quite severe pain would instantly vanish, teaching me once again that my mind holds unbelievable power over my body IF I let it. Eventually, I allowed myself the authority to declare, "We can clear our bodies of anything if we understand why we attracted the lesson/condition to us in the first place and are willing to clear it and let it go."

If I can impress anything on you, please take my word that you do not need to learn the same hard lesson over and over. I didn't need the three-zillion tumor-like headaches or the endless nights feeling sick with worry to remember that in the end I am powerful, and I can heal my own life. Nowadays, I remember to drop into my heart and fall through the fear, dancing my way down and feeling it all. This process can be undeniably uncomfortable and awful, but the fear clears as I descend and there, in that place, I always feel and know the truth. I am never alone, because I am Love, and I am Loved.

The week following the Rainbow Dream had been emotionally taxing, with the panic attacks and the waiting for the MRI results, but I woke up on the seventh day feeling different. I felt that the cancer was gone.

I sat around pondering for a couple of days, aware that my next dose of chemo was due to be given soon and that I was scheduled for another three-month course followed by radiotherapy. That feeling I'd had pre-C when I knew I was ill without having any visible outward symptoms was just as strong now. This time, I'd learned all I needed, cleared everything sticky, felt everything stuck, and wowzers, Bob's your bloomin' uncle and Fanny's your aunt, I was C-free!

If I needed further proof that my instincts were right, I noticed my hair had begun to grow back. The doctors hadn't scheduled it to grow back until *after* all the treatment had ended. Well, my body had obviously listened to them for once and knew that according to the body-clock calendar, my treatment HAD ended! I knew I was better, but I now had to convince the Men in White of that fact. You can imagine how my assertion went down.

"I know it's what you'd like to believe," said Dr. White Coat, giving me a politician-like smile, "but last week's scan still shows that you have tumours."

"I know I'm right, you'll have to scan me again."

"Karen, we can't keep exposing you to unnecessary radiation.

Let's just finish this round off and then we'll reassess. How does that sound?" He gave me the cheerful smile of someone who has never had to go through this kind of treatment

I began to sense the emotion I now recognized as ANGER and tried to express my feelings calmly. It didn't work. It would have been so easy to give-up at this point and passively accede to the direction of someone who believed themselves to be the authority. But, instead of allowing myself to be suppressed, I began to connect with the part of myself who had spent the last six months learning that she no longer had to be a silent good girl and *could* make a fuss without worrying what people thought about her.

"NO WAY. SCAN ME NOW, OR I AM WALKING OUT AND NOT COMING BACK!"

Nurses were summoned to soothe the situation, but nobody was really listening to me. The fear of powerlessness forced me to control my outburst and calmly explain to deaf ears for a final time why I knew I was healed. Knowing consultants like physical proof instead of feelings, I pointed to my head and began to explain the facts.

"Your hair is growing back?" the doctor repeated incredulously.

"Yes…" By this time, I was even starting to doubt myself.

Forcing back one of the most patronizing smiles I have ever seen, Doctor White Coat changed tactics and tried to quiet me by laying on the fear, guilt, and shame. "Because you still have visible tumors, the only way of really knowing if the cancer is active or not is to send you to London for a PET scan, and they are *so expensive.* Plus, you'd need to be injected with a radioactive tracer, which would mean Connor wouldn't be able to see you for twenty-four hours after. You need to be sensible and think about your son in all this." I swear he had a smug look on his face as he said that last part.

"BOOK ME IN!" I haughtily insisted.

One PET scan later and I was summoned to the hospital. Strangely (or perhaps not), the consultant I usually saw was not there. Instead, a Junior White Coat reported, "There is no explanation for this, but it seems you were right. Despite having large palpable tumors in the last MRI, this scan shows that you don't have a single active cancer cell in your body."

I'd like to say I was gracious at this point, but I think I sniffed something snooty about maybe actually listening to a patient rather than a textbook next time.

And that really was the end of the illness; healing one day, healed the next. Over the course of the next week, the tennis-ball sized "lumps" vanished, and I was now free to be myself.

I want to let you in on a little secret about healing. In the beginning, my desperation to fix myself meant I over-complicated things. I'd pray whilst holding sacred crystals, visualize wellness whilst sitting in ice-cold baths, sing affirmations whilst bouncing on a trampoline (I kid you not!), and tried various strict cancer diets with endless coffee enemas.

I am not saying these things don't have benefit; I'm saying that the answers to what you need won't come as easily from this place of fear. You don't have to search into the depths of your soul to drag up the painful past—in fact, the more you can relax and be gentle with yourself, the better this works. You simply must be willing to *let go and trust*. I appreciate that isn't always an easy thing to do when fear is breathing down your neck and hospital appointments and decisions are due, but from this place anything that needs to heal will float to the surface, towards the light you are allowing to shine.

This next part takes a little bit more trust and is something that I still have to work on reminding myself from time to time. When feelings of pain do dance your way, instead of running away and distracting yourself, take a big deep breath and FEEL. Dropping into this dark place is where you can find the deepest gold!

The final part of the magical spell-like process, which I still need to return to every day if I am to remain balanced, is to be in nature, even if this is just sitting next to a tree in a city park for fifteen minutes during a lunch break. During my time of "illness," no matter what was happening on the outside I found time to lay upon the ground, often for hours. I walked barefoot when I could and felt the nourishment of Mother Earth seep into my body, helping me to heal.

My willingness to heal emboldened my Trust, which then led me to open and allow the pain to flow through me. The pain, dancing its way back to the earth, led me to the roots of it all, Bliss. And, at the root of Bliss lies all that there is: LOVE.

Since I was told that I would most likely be infertile after the chemo, it came as no surprise to find out that I was pregnant six months later. It also came as no surprise that they couldn't explain that either. They tenaciously tried to prepare me to expect a deformed baby, saying the toxic chemo drugs would have damaged the DNA development of the fetus. One doctor even advised me to consider a termination. I knew they were wrong and told them as much, and fourteen years later my daughter Freya remains to be one of the strongest and most lovely people I know. The doctors declared her a one-off miracle until a year later when I became pregnant with my gorgeous twins, and then the real fun adventure began.

I have come to trust that we already know what we need in life, but sometimes just need a little reminder. Divine timing always nudges us towards the perfect person or situation in order to help us grow.

I cannot tell this story without writing my gratitude to

Kim, who I mentioned earlier in the chapter. I was at my lowest ebb when I met her, but with a laugh that is belly-deep and connects you to her heart, she spoke of Mother Earth so beautifully that her Truth sparked a memory with the Love I had always known within my heart, and I began to wake up to my own voice.

I didn't know what an empowered woman was until I met Kim. She once said to me, "The deeper you fall into your pain, the deeper you fall into Love." It took me a while to understand her meaning, but it remains today one of the wisest things I know and is the key to a Blissful life on earth.

Today I am happy, empowered, and gain wisdom with each passing day. Even in the dark times, I can play in the shadows of sadness and yet still feel pockets of bliss.

My cancer wasn't random. It may have been scary at the beginning when I didn't understand it, but it truly was a dark gift. I found that I didn't die if I showed my fear or screamed out in anger. I realized I didn't have to carry other people's emotional baggage, that it was possible to sink into the heart of pain and find Love, and that humor and playfulness could still be present even on the darkest days. It was the wildest way my body knew to wake me up and force me to listen to my instincts. It literally offered me the ability to stand in my own power, to express what I was feeling without worrying about what other people thought, and to move forward and claim the life I wanted.

I am no longer hurt by other people's judgements because I now realize that they belong to them alone; it is only their fear talking, because they haven't yet learned to be responsible for their own feelings.

I learned that I have always had everything inside me that I've ever needed; the little girl within, who still today dances "in and out of the dusky bluebells," is the part of my soul who urges me to remember my connection to the earth and to my own healing abilities. Being empowered means that I now listen (most of the time, at least) and trust that the Universe has my back, leaving me free to play in nature and in Love.

As much as I love all of nature, I believe Divine timing played a part in the reason we moved to the midlands when I was ill so that my husband, son, and I could find our own patch of Heaven. Calke Abbey is a National Trust estate in Derbyshire where I rediscovered the simple Joy of my childhood, and fairies *really do* live here. To this day, it remains a place of Love and is so special in my family's heart as the place where anything is possible, and where magic happens.

I can't explain why some places feel lighter and more powerful than others, but there is a "pull" at Calke and a great feeling of holding. It is a place you can go with hundreds of visitors and still find space to be blessedly alone. And yes, it's Bliss because there are roses and bluebells and rare wild orchids, and lakes, and wildlife, and beautiful ancient trees. God somehow feels closer at Calke.

My hope for any reader who resonates with my story and who may currently be dealing with physical or emotional disease is that you are able to find your own special place in nature and remember how exceptional you are. There is not another person who has ever lived that is exactly like you or faced your exact set of challenges. You are NOT a statistic in a medical journal; you are your own special brand of unique healing potential. Be gentle with yourself, be kind to yourself, and put yourself at the center of your life.

No one knows the answers to what you need, not even me, but I can promise you this: when you breathe into this Loving space, the panic slows down, hope starts to dance, fear starts to dissipate, and as if by magic you'll effortlessly find the answers which are right for YOU.

About Karen McGinty

Karen is a happily married mum of four who worked as a nurse in a busy emergency department in England. Her personal journey through a life-threatening illness in 2001 brought about a spiritual awakening and gave her the opportunity to face long-hidden painful emotions, which led to finding her own healing potential and bringing about a deeper connection to Love.

Healing gave her the power to listen to and trust her own intuition, and so in-between having babies and wanting more family time to homeschool, she left the NHS and studied Bowen therapy and harmonic healing and trained as a grief therapist.

Karen has a deep love of the natural world and now wants to combine the restorative benefits of nature with clients who are struggling to work through painful emotions. She has a passion for helping empower other people to face long-buried emotions and free themselves so they can have a brighter, healthier, and more playful future. In her spare time, she enjoys writing, drinking scrumptious coffee, playing with her children, and barefoot dancing in the forest.

Email: Karenmcginty71@gmail.com
Instagram: @Belleamebooks
Facebook: Belle Âme Books

2

Being Authentically, Unapologetically YOU!

by Lia Venet

Being Authentically, Unapologetically YOU!

Today, people look at me and see a happy, free spirit and an authentic woman who radiates joy. What they don't know is what it took to get here: a lot of work on self-growth.

I grew up in Chicago with the good old "Midwest values": **work hard** (rewarded for busyness), always take care of others first (programmed in women especially), **be modest** (don't shine too brightly or stand out), remember that **"your word is your bond"** (a lot of "shoulds" in these words), **always lend a helping hand** (a recipe for over-giving), **treat your name and reputation as your most prized possession** (leads to perfectionism and caring too much about what others think of you), and **don't stand out** (leads to dimming your brightness). After a few years of growing up under these terms, it became clear to me that I had a strong, resistant, and resilient soul that refused to let my body do anything that didn't resonate with my spirit. In short, the values with did not align with my soul's purpose. This simple conflict generated many life struggles and challenges that have now transformed into the gifts that I have today. By sharing what I have learned, I hope to help others become who they truly are, and who they are meant to be.

For as long as I can remember, I had an overwhelming feeling that I didn't belong, even within my own family. Don't get me wrong, I love my family and they love me. However, I was the one that was a bit different—the black sheep. I wanted to talk openly about my feelings and be truthful about being my authentic self, but that just seemed to make everyone uncomfortable. My sensitivity did not fit into the space that my family had made for me. I also struggled to fit in with my peers in elementary school; I had friends, but I wasn't one of the popular kids. I was shy and drawn to the "misfits," the ones that were different.

My mother was a "good Midwest woman" who put everyone before herself and never spoke about her dreams, struggles, or feelings. They were all locked neatly inside for so many years, stacking up layer upon layer. I remember many times as a small child being told by my maternal grandparents, who lived with us, to be quiet because my mother had a migraine. I would quietly walk into her dark room and watch her lying with an icepack on her head. I felt so sorry for her and wanted her to be well. I always felt that I needed to protect my fragile mommy; I needed to be strong. This feeling carried into my adult life, which revealed itself as a tendency to over-give to others and not be willing to receive.

My father was also a "good Midwest man." He never called in sick, worked hard, and conformed to society as a good citizen. When he retired, he received a street sign with his name on it instead of a gold watch for his "hard work" after all of those years of service.

I grew up in a white neighborhood with strict, conforming values that were steeped in segregation. In fact, my maiden name is *Caamaño*, but the tilde was dropped to hide that it was a Hispanic name. You see, if you were a Hispanic in my neighborhood, you were called a "spic" unless you lived in a suburb and said you were Spanish, NOT Mexican. People assumed I was Italian, even my best friend Wendy that I had known since I was two. I didn't dare tell them anything else for fear of being called a "spic" and having no friends, especially because the Hispanic kids wouldn't accept me because I was white. Desegregation only started when I was in seventh and eighth grade. Black people were bused from the south side of Chicago to the white schools in our northwest side of the city, but whites and blacks did not talk. Looking back it made no sense, but fear has a way of encouraging secrets. What I now know to be true is that when you speak the truth, it can no longer hide in the darkness. You don't have to hold these secrets inside of you, and if you do, they will eventually make you physically and emotionally sick. Speaking the truth can be uncomfortable, but the more you practice the easier it becomes.

I grew up with two brothers, one older and one younger. My older brother turned into a heroin addict and constantly extorted money from my grandparents and parents. He once stole their car and then sold it back to them, and they bought it! I was dumbstruck. Even then, I could see the bigger picture and didn't understand why no one else around me could. Why did they keep giving him money? It would be so much better for my brother if the adults would give him some "tough love," but the old patterns of dysfunction were playing out in our family.

One day, when I was fifteen years old, my older brother pulled a knife on my boyfriend just because he didn't like him. I warned my brother three times that he better put the knife away or I was going to call the police. When he didn't back down, I carried out my threat. The police came, and they took my brother to the station because he smarted off to them. As they were leaving, my grandfather came up to me, looked me in the eyes, and pointed his finger at me while saying, "How could you do that to your own brother!" It felt like that knife had gone straight through my heart. I felt so shamed and so unloved. Then, one of the police officers who had seen what just happened whispered in my ear, "Honey, you need to get out of here."

This moment was a turning point in my life. It was the first time that an adult authority from outside of my family witnessed the craziness that was going on and said something to me. That policeman was an angel in disguise. The experience planted a seed in me that secretly told me there was something more out there—that this was not the only way people live.

I got a job at a travel agency in Chicago a couple of years later when I was seventeen years old. Filing away brochures for various destinations was my portal into another world. My eyes were opened to so many places that I wanted to experience, and I started to dream about all the places I wanted to go. This was a new interest and awareness for me, and I felt my world start to expand.

I had never even been on an airplane until I met a skydiver and went up to watch him jump when I was sixteen. Sitting on the floor next to the pilot of the small Cessna with no seat or seat belt, I observed as the three skydivers climbed over me to jump out. I leaned my head out to watch them fall away from the plane and the pilot asked me to put my head back inside—I guess I was making him nervous. I was fascinated though. I used to watch the Golden Knights jump into the Chicago airshow every year and thought you had to be chosen. Now I find out that you can just jump out of planes? I wanted to do that!

I will never forget July 21, 1985, the day of my first jump. I was nineteen years old. I felt a combination of nervousness and excitement from the moment I woke up all the way until I let go of the plane. The anticipation was the hardest part for me; once my hands let go of the plane I felt myself free in the sky, immersed in the moment. It was a moving meditation where I felt every single second of pure freedom. Then, when I opened my parachute, it was so quiet and peaceful. Looking down at my black student boots dangling beneath me, I screamed with joy, "I'm flying!" No one could hear me or see the vitality, the freedom, and the joy that I was feeling. As soon as I landed safely on the ground, I wanted to go right back up again. I was hooked! This was the beginning of my ten-year skydiving career. It was an expensive habit, but it was worth every penny. It introduced me to a new way of living that came from a place of trusting my soul, stepping out of conformity, and living from a new normal that made me feel alive.

When I started skydiving, my world opened even more. I met people from many different countries that had unique perspectives on life. It was the first time I found a group of people that could see a bigger picture in life, and these people became my second family. I felt like I could be myself there more than anywhere else. I ended up dating my first skydiving instructor and moved to Reno to live with him for about two years before we broke up.

I attended the University of Nevada, Reno for a bachelor's degree in business administration, although I almost quit in my last year because I had to give presentations in every class and was afraid to speak in front of so many people. Throughout this time, I wanted to move to California so that I could be closer to the Skydance Skydiving Dropzone in Davis and not have to drive through the Sierra Mountains every weekend.

After graduating, I quit my two jobs, stored my belongings, and took a three-month backpacking trip through Europe, travelling with a dear friend for the first two weeks before heading off on my own. I experienced fifteen countries during that trip while embracing the adventures of the unknown. This is the secret sauce! If you can take leaps of faith, trust yourself and trust life without knowing what's going to happen, and let go of that false sense of security that we get when we don't leap, *that's* when the magic begins. I'm not talking about being "reckless," just living five percent out of your comfort zone most of the time so you can experience vibrancy, trust, and living life to the fullest.

After coming back from my trip, I found a place to live in California and started working two jobs. I always liked to have multiple streams of income so I didn't have all my eggs in one basket, so to speak. This gave me a sense of freedom because I always had a choice and never felt stuck. My first two jobs in California were at a travel agency in Davis and at FedEx in Oakland. Both had travel benefits, which was a requirement for me and my new-found hobby! I probably would have been a gypsy my whole life if I hadn't met my soul mate, Philippe Venet, while I was skydiving in 1991 shortly after returning from my European backpacking trip. It's funny, because I told my friend that I would never date a French guy because I foolishly believed the generalization that French people are rude due to a one-time experience in France. Those small-minded comments always come back to bite us, although this time it was in a good way. Since Philippe was French, he always stood out, which meant I could easily hide behind him so that I didn't have to take up space—a comfortable pattern from my past that I didn't even see until ten years into my marriage. We were very different in many ways, but we both had a love for the sky. We competed in the 1994 US National Skydiving competition on a four-way skydiving team after training together for a year, and we came in sixth place out of twenty-five teams. We got married that same year and started our family right away, with our son *Téva* arriving in 1995 and our daughter Ange-Elise in 1997.

My next leap of faith and trust was being a stay-at-home mom for twenty years. It sounded so old-fashioned, and I heard so many people say that you give up so much to do this and that it wasn't a wise choice. However, my deep knowing was in alignment with taking this risk, even though it was a bit scary for my independent personality. I have never regretted this decision—well, there were a few times that I threatened to get a job, but for the most part Philippe valued what I was doing for our children and our family. Throughout those twenty years, there were so many lessons for me on dependency, communication, boundaries, standing up for myself, speaking my truth, and valuing myself even when it felt like society did not value what I was doing. I remember being at social parties and having someone ask, "What do you do?" When I replied that I was a stay-at-home mom, they didn't know what to say. I could feel the awkwardness and internalized the story that I wasn't valued, a story that I had to consciously change.

During these years, there were so many opportunities for growth as we played out the patterns from our ancestors. One thing that I learned along the way is that even if one person in a relationship is doing the self-growth work, then it is still possible to have a happy marriage. You see, while I was the one who did all of this work, my husband directly benefited from it as well. Over the years, he has become a very "Zen man" compared to being the "no man" who used to yell, a pattern he had learned from his father. Once I learned to be the "calm in the chaos" when he defaulted to this pattern and not participating in it, there was no one for him to pull into these arguments and our children learned how to deal with him and with other people that behave like this. I recognize that it might not always work, but at least if you try and your partner doesn't elevate with you, he will organically fall away and you will be left no regrets because you did everything that you could. As part of this growth, I have required taking time away for me and time away for us in addition to insisting on having uncomfortable conversations when necessary. Looking back, this was a great habit for self-care and couple care.

Over these twenty-five years of marriage, one of the most important things that I contribute to us still being together is that I was always willing to have uncomfortable conversations with him. It's not that I like to have them, it's just that my soul needs to stay in integrity. I knew from watching my mother suppressing her feelings, frequently being sick, and constantly having this air of melancholy surrounding her that I had to do things differently in my marriage—I was going to do everything I could not to suppress my feelings and let them accumulate like my mother did.

One example of a more recent uncomfortable conversation occurred when our son was going to college and our daughter was a senior in high school. I was taking courses to become a Health Coach, Life Coach, and entrepreneur, and I didn't want to have to cook all the time—a set pattern that we had been doing for the last fifteen years. My husband said it was okay if I didn't cook, but energetically I could tell that it wasn't. One day, he slammed the refrigerator door and said there was nothing to eat before storming out. I lost it! I was so upset, I started to leave the house and fell to the floor in the garage crying. There was nowhere to go; I had to BE with ME and the uncomfortableness of what my soul was trying to tell me. I had to be willing to leave behind everything if I was going to speak up for myself. I knew that I had to, or I would be miserable. It was so uncomfortable, not knowing if I was going to lose everything—my partner, my house, my security—but deep down I knew I would always be okay.

When Phillipe returned, I told him that I didn't want to cook, clean, and do the same job that I have had while our kids were home. I wanted to start to do other work in the world as a Life Coach, helping empower women, and if he wasn't okay with this then it wasn't fair to either of us to remain together. He said, "You can't just quit. I can't quit my job." And I said, "Why not? Says who? If you want to, we can figure out another plan." From then on, our relationship has changed. He really has accepted this new way of life, and he doesn't expect me to cook or clean all the time. I can see how I could have been afraid to share that with him because I might have lost my security, but what good is security in being miserable?

In November of 2016, I jumped onboard KC Baker's WomanSpeak vision right at its inception. At the time, I had no idea how powerful this global movement would be. The members of my WomanSpeak circles have said that they have gotten more confidence, clarity, and connection to themselves as well as to each other through this community. It can be hard to find other women that are doing this deep work of self-growth, but WomanSpeak attracts women that are committed to investing in themselves with time and money. The culture is one of non-judgement and non-comparison; one of fertile listening and celebrating each other. Women want to be seen and celebrated, not fixed and critiqued. The sixteen-month curriculum has a monthly theme and focuses on the energetics of public speaking, using feminine practices to get yourself into your body before you speak because that's where our deepest wisdom lies.

The women who come to these circles are all different ages, different cultures, and different backgrounds. What they have in common is that they are all leaders who want to make a difference in the world. Some women arrive knowing what their core message is, and some women arrive not knowing at all. No matter where you are right now, WomanSpeak provides a safe place to explore the depths of your heart and soul, and you never know what you'll uncover. There are lots of hidden gifts that you will never know that you have unless you invest in yourself. It's so much fun as a facilitator to watch women blossom into their brilliance right before my eyes. Not only do they get to practice speaking, but they also practice listening and reflection when celebrating each woman that is speaking. It changes the way these women are showing up in all areas of their life. Who doesn't like a person that can really listen and hear what we're saying, and then reflect back the beauty that they see in you?

Today I am leading two WomanSpeak circles in Livermore, Northern California. I organize and facilitate four-day empowerment beach retreats called "Rise Together Sisters" for women leaders in the Santa Cruz area, and I also have HeartMind Virtual Circles that provide women leaders a safe place to be seen, heard, and supported in taking the next steps towards what they desire in their personal and professional lives. I also take limited one-on-one clients that want to be supported in becoming more courageous in stepping into the life that they truly desire from a place of adventure under any situation.

When I first joined WomanSpeak, I said yes to being a facilitator but not to being a speaker. At that time, I thought that I wasn't a speaker—remember that I almost quit college because of my fear of presentations? However, what I have learned through all of the curriculum and experience is that I *am* a speaker; in fact, we ALL are speakers in our lives. Whether it is on a public stage, at your work, or in your relationships with your parents, partners, children, friends, or boss, YOU are a speaker. And if you can learn how to speak powerfully and effectively so that others can really hear what you're saying, then you can make so much more of an impact in your life and in the lives of others as well.

Are you speaking your truth? Or, do you sometimes hold back because you're not sure if others will judge you? Does a little voice in your head say, "Who am I to say that?" Many times it feels easier and more comfortable to hold it in and not say anything, but is it really? Is holding in our beliefs and messages helping us, or anyone else? What stops us from sharing these messages, ideas, and thoughts that we believe in so deeply?

I see so many women that live mediocre lives because they are conforming to the old ways of putting everyone else first. They don't have the courage to say yes to themselves and be authentically who they are because they fear judgement from the world around them. They watch others on Facebook living their happy lives instead of living their own fully, telling themselves that the people they are seeing are just lucky. Their focus is outward instead of inward. They are waiting for someone else to give them what they haven't given themselves. They don't want to be uncomfortable, so they hold that voice inside of them, the one that their soul is nudging to speak up.

I see the gifts that you have, and I see the brilliance in you—why can't you see it in yourself? If only you would believe that on the other side of being uncomfortable is lightness and empowerment. If you only knew that if you took care of yourself first, you would have so much more energy to do so much more. If only you knew that you can do it, and that you didn't have to do it alone. If only you knew how many others were waiting for YOU to show them the way with your unique gifts. I am so grateful to be part of a global movement that is providing women the space and opportunity to step into their greatness and to rewire their neuro-pathways so that they can speak their truth with confidence and clarity in a way that can be heard by others.

One of the problems we must combat to truly be able to

speak our truth is ridding ourselves of the old paradigms. For example, one of my strong beliefs is, "I believe that women need to take care of themselves first before taking care of others." When I say this out loud in a group of women, it brings up all kinds of old programming and defensiveness in some of them. This programming makes us default to making up excuses why we don't put ourselves first, such as, "Oh, well you're just lucky because you're married and have a nice husband." This then triggers me to be concerned about how I am making them uncomfortable, and as a result I may decide to hold some things in that I really wanted to say.

The word paradigm has become a buzzword in the emerging world; there is lots of talk about old and new paradigms. The word "paradigm" comes from the Greek word *paradeigma*, meaning an example, a model, or a pattern.

For many of us, the old paradigm operates under fear, doubt, worry, judgment, comparison, limited thinking, and feelings that we are not enough, all created by a patriarchal structure that values males above females. In this patriarchal structure, male-brain thinking—which tends to be penetrating, linear, and focused communication—is valued above the female brain, which is discounted as being too wordy, too emotional, all over the place, not to the point, and more. However, the female brain is brilliant in its own unique way, spiraling and gathering all kinds of information in no order and popping out a big "wisdom bomb" at the end that makes people's jaws drop. Physically, female brains have verbal centers on both sides of the brain while males tend to have verbal centers on only the left hemisphere. Both brains are equally valuable for different reasons. This is not taught in the old paradigm, and in my opinion it is important to teach this to the next generation so they can evolve into the new paradigm. One way that this is being taught right now is to women in WomanSpeak Circles globally, and GirlSpeak Circles will be starting soon to teach this same message to high school girls.

The truth is that when women commit to themselves by investing time and money into their self-growth, they take the lead in their own life as well as for all their loved ones around them by becoming FULL-filled and modelling what a fully-expressed women looks and feels like. Each woman that does this creates a ripple effect for all the women around her, inspiring them to be who they authentically are, and *that* is how we are going to change the world—one person at a time. It's not easy work, but when you become fulfilled you will radiate joy, happiness, and the courage to step into the unknown, inspiring others to do the same.

There are three core teachings that I hope you take away from this chapter: taking care of yourself first before caring for others, looking inward for validation instead of outside, and having a willingness to be uncomfortable so that you can stay in integrity with your soul. I also hope that you have learned the benefits of consistently surrounding yourself with like-hearted women that listen deeply to each other so that you each feel fully seen and understood—a community that supports each other with no judgement or comparison, only deep listening and celebration. If you remember nothing else, please remember these four things to help you DARE to BE Full-filled:

1. **Say YES to yourself before others** and you will have the energy to give so much more. Happiness is an inside job. We teach other people how to treat us, so treat yourself like a queen. Don't expect others to give to you what you aren't willing to give to yourself; if you wait for others to give you what you want, it will never

be enough. Only you can give yourself what you need. Practice setting healthy boundaries.

2. **Look internally for your answers instead of externally.** Be aware of when you are caring too much about what other people think of you. When you make your decisions in life based on the opinions of others, you're giving your power away and are out of "soul integrity."

3. **Be willing to be uncomfortable**. Speak from your heart while having necessary conversations, speaking up for your needs, and setting healthy boundaries. Take action to stand up for your soul by speaking, being, or doing something that goes against the norms of conformity, even when it appears that others might be judging you for doing so.

4. **You don't have to do it alone.** It is empowering to be witnessed when speaking vulnerably from your heart by a community of other like-hearted women that are saying yes to themselves first, are looking internally for answers, and are willing to be uncomfortable. This vision is already created in WomanSpeak by founder KC Baker, and we are spreading rapidly. It's fun to find our voices in a circle with other women, and it's so much more sustainable than trying to do it alone. You can invest in yourself by becoming a member or earn commission as a facilitator of a WomanSpeak Circle. For more information go to: www.WomanSpeak.com

When I was growing up, there was no time or space to be sensitive; no room to be different or to stand out from the norm. And yet, this was my foundation which helped me to become who I am today. I have broken through those chains of the ancestral ways that bonded my family; those rigid beliefs that things must be done in a certain way. Through the uncomfortableness of being the black sheep, I broke through the patterns that fought to hold me back. I thought that being a rebel was a negative word back then, but today I see it as a courageous act of living your truth by not conforming simply because you want to fit in. Once my eyes were opened, I started to dream and see unlimited possibilities and I started to create my life the way I wanted it to be. Once you start to see what is possible, you truly can make anything happen.

I have followed my soul's calling, and you can too. Follow your heart (your inner knowing) instead of your head (your ego). When you can use your head's intelligence in service of your heart and your soul, that's when you're in harmony, alignment, and soul integrity.

About Lia Venet

Lia Venet is known for living life to the fullest. Over the course of ten years she has made 1,400 skydives, 100 of which were with her son in utero. Today, she supports women in jumping out of their comfort zone and leaping into a life of authentic adventure.

Besides her PhD in life experience, Lia is a Certified Holistic Health and Transformational Coach. Whether it's teaching workshops, holding circles, or mentoring other women as the need arises, she welcomes the opportunity to help other women to "be FULL-filled" and happy from the inside out. She holds space for women to speak their truths and explore their ideas, thoughts, and messages in a safe space in her WomanSpeak Circles and leads a four-day beach retreat called Rise Together Sisters for women leaders to go deeper in courageously becoming more of their authentic self. She also created and facilitates a virtual HeartMind (a feminine mastermind for women to rise together), is a co-author of a 365 Days of Gratitude book, and is an authentic speaker who shares from the heart.

Married to her soulmate Philippe for twenty-five years with two amazing grown children that are making huge differences in the world, Lia resides in Northern California with Philippe and their golden retriever Max.

www.womanspeak.com/lvenet/
www.liavenet.com
Facebook: Lia Venet

3

From Straitjacket Bound to Success

by Holly Chadwick

From Straitjacket Bound
to Success

As I'm making the documentary *Music in My Head*—featuring my mother, myself, and mental illness—I've come to realize that what I'm focusing on in this film is my own story. It's a story that even as I write it here, I am afraid that it will come with a stigma attached. However, I believe that the wisdom I gained from my rather wild story of promise, of perils, and ultimately of conquering mental illness is important to share as it provides an example of how to live an authentic and creative life.

When I first started working on this documentary, I actually thought the story would be more about my mother. She is schizophrenic and has moved from paranoid delusions, violent acts, and hearing voices to living with music in her head. She is referred to as "the walking jukebox" by her neighbours in the small community she lives in as she has auditory hallucinations of both original music and songs she has heard on the radio. I thought the documentary would simply profile how she has managed the scary symptoms of schizophrenia and how she lives with the constant music. Over time, however, the story shifted to my own experiences with mental illness—both my mother's and my own.

Her illness has affected me drastically. Because my mom was deemed unable to safely care for a child, I was raised by my grandparents from birth. However, there were a few scary years where my mother was living with us. Her paranoid delusions would tell her to throw me out of the dining room window, or even to come at me with knives. In these moments, I would always run to the forest and hide. However, having some weird loyalty and understanding of her situation, I would never tell on her.

I quickly learned to identify what was real and unreal. To my mom, her delusions were real. To me, as a kid, the dragon lady she saw in the dining room china hutch was pretend. Sometimes, though, my mom *became* the violent dragon lady and chased me around the dining room table, and I had to get away quickly. That was not pretend. I had to read the smallest of signs that may signal one of my mom's psychotic episodes, and I think that this experience really made me interested in the world of make believe, and ultimately in storytelling. We went on like this until around the time I was in the second grade.

My father was a Vietnam vet, and he didn't live with us as my grandparents didn't accept him as part of the family. One night he fell asleep while smoking in his Seattle apartment, and he was burned so badly that he had to wear a mask to keep his face intact and hide the burns. I was told he was dead, but after my grandparents passed away when I was twenty-five I found out he actually lived for another year before succumbing to a heart attack. Weirdly, since I considered him a part of the family, I had continued drawing him in family pictures at school until he actually died—while his passing went unannounced, I must have instinctually felt that it had happened. Or, maybe I heard talk of his death through the heating vents while I was alone in my room at night.

When my father finally died, my mom had her last psychotic episode in our home. As she was hurling hefty ceramic busts at my grandparents, the police came and took her away. When I saw her later in the hospital she apologized to me profusely, although I didn't understand why. I also didn't recognize this creature in front of me with the flat, medicated personality. The mom I knew was gone.

As soon as my mom was hospitalized, my grandparents

got me a cocker spaniel, who I named Charlie, and put me in piano lessons. I loved that dog, and I took to piano like I was breathing for the first time. I practiced piano non-stop, and from the very start I was making up my own music. I would play for my grandfather late into the night, with Charlie at my side and a hot fire blazing in the wood stove. There were many stories running through my head, ones that felt very real to me, and I would pour them into my music. I articulated the drama going on with my mother through the notes I played. I would conjure visions of my dog and I going on adventures in the forest and playing ball with Grandpa in the yard.

As I got older, I felt drawn to bring the stories in my head onto the TV screen—I had always turned to movies and television shows as a grand distraction from my own life. *The Brady Bunch* was the perfect family to live up to, and boy we were far from that! I also became obsessed with sci-fi shows because they attempted to normalize the unreal. I could relate to aliens of *Star Trek* and monsters of the week on *The X-Files*, and they made me forget about my stressful family life.

Driven to not be like my mother, I excelled at school—my grandparents never had to tell me to do my homework. I was talented at music, writing, and the visual arts, so English and literature were my favourite classes. When I was sixteen my neighbour Lynn took notice of my talents and hired me to do filing and faxing for the healthcare recruiting business she ran out of her home. Once she realized that I was good at computers too, she had me design her website and digitize her filing cabinet full of physician resumes. We quickly figured out that hospitals were willing to pay for this information, and so the first healthcare-centered online job board was born. I was a dot-com entrepreneur before I had even graduated from high school!

After high school I went away on scholarship to the University of California at Santa Cruz and studied film and digital media. Lynn would fly me back during my summer breaks to make website changes, handle emails, and manage partnerships with tech and marketing companies. By the time I graduated, I had a keen business sense, real-world experience, and a new degree in something I loved. I thought the whole world was my oyster—that is, until my grandfather had a stroke on the day of my graduation ceremony.

Instead of staying in California and leveraging my experience and degree into working at a Silicon Valley media company, I came home to deal with my grandparents both falling ill. My grandma was developing dementia and had congestive heart failure, and neither of them had much time left. Being the dutiful granddaughter that I was, I went with my grandmother to the care home my grandpa was in every day until he died. I tried my best to care for my grandmother, but when her dementia took a mean turn and she started coming at me with knives, I knew that this was something I couldn't live with. I had to get out. I fled to live with my cousins in Canada while nurses kept a watchful eye on my grandma, and meals were delivered to her daily. It hurt me deeply to leave her, but I had to wait until she was frail enough to put her in a care home.

While I was living in Canada, I made a few comedy movies with people I had met at a Vancouver Film School directing class. They were a great distraction and gave me some real-world film experience.

In a matter of weeks my grandmother had one too many falls and began turning weird shades of yellow, so it was time to put her in a care home. As I left her in the facility she yelled at me that my "goose was cooked," and I did my best to ignore her foreboding message. I was finally my own person, with nothing but my own future ahead of me. Or so I thought.

When my grandmother died, my estranged mom did not take the news well. At this time she was living on her own, but she was off her meds and out of the mental health system and she couldn't keep it together. She became an alcoholic, and I started getting calls from her at 2:00 a.m. asking me to pick her up at the local 7-11. She also was about to be evicted from her apartment. I had to tell her to get her act together or she'd be homeless; I wouldn't have let that happen, but I had to make her believe it.

After all these years, I was suddenly her caregiver and had to face having a relationship with her again. As a result, I discovered that I was not doing well at all.

The week after my grandmother's funeral, I had a Thanksgiving party planned. It was the first time in a couple years that I would see my friends from college, so I had been looking forward to it. However, the grief of losing my grandparents and the stress of dealing with my mother was just too much, and by the time the party came around I hadn't slept in several days. After everyone left, I lost it big time.

I found myself in the fetal position in the back of my grandpa's car as my college friend drove me to the hospital, hearing music in my head. I was terrified that I had become my mother. My friend told me to sing along to the radio, which was playing Bjork's "All is Full of Love." I belted out the lyrics over and over again as we drove, trying to contradict the beautiful, surreal music that was simultaneously playing in my head. My mind was playing tricks on me. Mathematical equations were beginning to collide with the music. I didn't know what was real and what was not; the lines between the two seamless. I was delusional. I *was* my mother.

When we got to the hospital, the nurses didn't know what to do with me. As I lay in the hospital bed, my friend told me to hold her hand and squeeze whenever my mind was scaring me. I squeezed her hand a lot that night. We eventually went home later that night once I had calmed down; this was a rural hospital on a remote island, ill-prepared to handle mental health symptoms. By morning, my aunt and cousins arrived at my home, having been called by my friend. When they first showed up, I truly thought that Santa had arrived on the roof with his reindeer. The photo of my grandparents next to my bed started melting before my eyes. I still hadn't slept.

I didn't have health insurance and my family was afraid to drive too far with unpredictable me in the car, so they took me back to the same hospital. The only solution the staff could come up with was to put me in a straitjacket. So as to not remember the visual for the future, I kept my eyes shut as I was put in the rather loose jacket, and then I was on an ambulance ride to a psych ward one county over. In the moment, though, I thought I was going to the starship Enterprise. Then, when I got there, I thought I was in some film school dorm and everyone there was an actor. I was never diagnosed with any official illness, and after spending a week at that ward I was discharged before Christmas with a new medication that I felt was very wrong and orders to get some rest.

I was lucky to stay for a week with a family friend, who happened to be a family counselor and understood mental health problems. A couple weeks later I had a wonderful Christmas with my family in Canada, and then a few weeks after that I was back in my grandparents' house. A couple weeks later, it was my birthday. I wasn't sleeping again, my medication wasn't working, I was hearing music in my head, and I thought the house was burning down. I fled the house barefoot in my pajamas and the newspaper delivery man picked me up. He thought I was high, so he took me to a trauma center for drug rehab. They quickly realized what was actually going on though, and I eventually made it back to that same psych ward.

I was there for another week, and I got on the right meds and got some much-needed rest. This time, I knew that I wasn't in the starship Enterprise or a film school dorm.

For the first time, I began to understand what my mom lives through on a daily basis. Even though I only got a glimpse of the music in my head, it gave me a much-needed perspective that allowed me to destroy the stigma I had created, build an appropriate connection with my mom, and ultimately forgive her. I now have a relationship with my mom that includes healthy boundaries. She is back in the mental health system and has caregivers coming in on a daily basis to help her around her apartment. I see her on a weekly basis, and we often have coffee and discuss the big questions: life after death, alien life, and why we're here on this planet.

My mom often asks me what the point of her life is, and for the longest time I didn't know how to answer her. I now know that the point of her life is for me to share her amazing struggle. As her daughter, it is my duty to share our stories with the world as insights. Being "mad," if only for a brief while, made me realize how dishabituating mental illness is. Often, the perception of someone with schizophrenia is that they just need to control their own thoughts and actions better, or that they're making excuses, or pretending, or lazy, or weak. I now know what it's like to be my mom after getting a glimpse into her world. I know how losing one's mind is the scariest thing that can happen. How you can't eat, sleep, or even do normal things such as having a conversation without second- or triple-guessing yourself. Even taking a bath can be scary—I literally thought I was on an aircraft carrier that was about to sink. How can you hold down a job and pay bills when you are paranoid and think that the shadows are out to get you? Mental illness is a terrifying sickness that takes over your mind, but just like my mom I learned how to overcome the scary parts. I spent so much time trying to not be like her, but with my unique insights, I'm now totally humbled and honoured for us to share this experience.

When I got out of the hospital, I started seeing an art therapist that I had grown close to while I was in treatment. Good meds and art therapy were the things that turned my life around. With her help and my drive not to permanently become my mother, I had a fire lit under my bum. I established a daily wellness regimen that included art, exercise, sleep, and good food that got me back to normalcy.

As a part of my new wellness regimen, I drove to Seattle on a weekly basis to take salsa lessons. As I became immersed in the music and culture, I learned to recognize what was real and unreal in my head and to detect something that may be becoming a bit off. Whenever I had a stray odd thought, or even music in my head, I literally salsa-ed along until it left. Having positive mantras also helped me dismiss scary thoughts. I would scream "I love puppies" in my head, or sometimes even out loud, to gain control over my thoughts. It may sound silly, but it worked! Discovering these techniques were part accident and part luck but mostly instinctual, and it really shouldn't have been this hard to discover what would work for me. As it turns out, most people never get very far in the recovery process because they can't find the right help.

With what seemed like baby steps, my mind got sharp enough for me to get a design job at a local photography magazine. I was still getting used to my medication, and I remember my mind feeling incredibly slow at first as I tried to navigate the computer. Eventually my mind got quicker and quicker, returning almost back to normal, and I continued to improve as I got married, became a puppy mom, started to teach kids photography, and got a new job at the local newspaper. Once I felt fully back to normal, I took a leap of faith and left my nine-to-five job at the newspaper to become an independent filmmaker.

As I grew bolder in my creative process, I explored post-traumatic stress disorder—a disorder I was all too familiar with—in my Amazon web series *Sounds of Freedom*. As a filmmaker, my story compelled me to write the character of Charlie, who is loosely based on my father. Doing this movie was a great first major project for me. I was able to fictionalize my own trauma and my ride with the newspaper delivery man. Living in a military community and absorbing their trauma helped me focus on the perils of veterans coming home from war. Exploring trauma as a theme through storytelling brought me closure to my own trauma.

With this project, I have attended film festivals all over the country and won many awards, including best director in the New York City Web Fest and best web series in the Philip K. Dick Film Festival. I now find myself working with a pitch coach and a casting director to prepare for a big meeting with Amazon in the new year to pitch a long-form version of my web series *Sounds of Freedom* as a Prime Original. I also have a journalist helping me make my documentary *Music in My Head*, and I have plans to make a narrative version of the documentary in the future.

Last year, there were two books that had a large impact on my life. On her deathbed, my mentor Lynn introduced me to Brené Brown's *Daring Greatly*, and I also discovered Arianna

Huffington's *Thrive* through a subscription to MentorBox. I was so wrapped up in these books' messages of authenticity and balanced living that I actually went to San Francisco in the Spring of 2018 to meet Jonathon Kendall and Alex Mehr of MentorBox in a round-table discussion where Alex invited investors to hear our start-up ideas. I was collaborating with Dave Richards, the founder of a technology company based in Portland, Oregon called RISEcx. This company had developed what they refer to as the "CareSpace Healthbot," which is designed to help patients interact with their healthcare in a new and more convenient way. Think of CareSpace as providing positive outcomes in the complex and clinical side of care through a relatable, unique, and thoughtful AI-powered health coach whose empathy goes far beyond what the healthcare industry is known for.

David and I both saw the potential for how CareSpace could assist patients with mental health conditions such as PTSD and depression—I wanted to make sure people didn't have to struggle as much as I did to get the right help. We also believed the series and documentary stories I am producing could provide much-needed therapy for mental health patients in a new, reimagined, interactive format that would be delivered through the CareSpace Healthbot. Instead of the traditional narrative documentary structure, CareSpace would adapt the story to tailor it to the individual patient based on the insights and understandings coming from artificial intelligence and machine learning. The Mentorbox round-table was useful in helping to develop the idea. Expect to hear more about this in 2019.

Recently, I have being approached to make more documentaries. I'm inspired to make the documentary called *A Dream and a Toolbox* that will cover a story that is the reason

I wanted to be a filmmaker in the first place. At the age of sixteen I went on a mission trip to Tijuana, Mexico. People in the slums lived in huts made out of mattresses and cardboard with corrugated metal roofs. They had no running water, yet they had a television. The amount of satellite dishes coming out from shanty roofs amazed me. As movies and television had been a great distraction from the trauma of my life, I realized that this was likely true for these people as well. This made me realize the importance of the storyteller's place in society and the effect of images on people, and I enrolled in film school a couple of years later. *A Dream and a Toolbox* will follow the story of a college student at a Seattle University going on a service trip to a war-torn country as a part of the organization Professionals Without Borders. It will also follow the story of a youth in the foreign county that benefits from this program—their life and circumstances and why they need help. When the two very different perspectives collide, magic happens! The images in their mind of each other, created by television, are dissolved, growth and revelations occur, and truths about friendship endure.

Today I have a consulting business called Wellness Creative Marketing, where I help healthcare and wellness professionals—from wellness authors and healthcare doctors to nutritionists, massage therapists, and yoga instructors—market themselves so they can find the right clients and help facilitate the same kind of wellness transformation that worked for me. Finding help should not be so hard for people in need. I spend my days planning films and structuring my business online.

I am happy and amazed to find myself going from a straitjacket to success in only fifteen short years. As I film my mother's daily life, as well as my own, I am amazed by our strength and determination.

Through much of this process, I've had the amazing support of my husband. He was there for me after my second hospital stay and has been with me for every step of the way. He has financially supported my movie projects as well as the fun and healthy lifestyle that allowed me to pivot into launching my marketing business. I hope I will be able to repay him one day by making millions on the silver screen or getting a six-figure income through my business.

Despite the obstacles that I faced, I trudged through my own mental illness, got support from a few wellness professionals, followed my passion, fell in love, and learned how to be successful. I enjoy living with my husband and two golden retrievers and taking our boat to the San Juans every summer.

People with mental health issues can lead authentic and healthy lives despite the odds. If you or someone you know has a mental illness, I hope my story of conquering my own stigma will instill in you the desire to at least shake hands with the stigma you've developed. Then, and only then, can other people's stigma be shaken. People struggling with mental illness can be very talented and creative, and with the right support they can have success in life and career. Moving past my brush with mental illness was a struggle, but by being brave and strategic and taking bold acts of faith, I conquered. It takes courage to live an authentic life, and it takes courage to share the story of my own personal struggle. If you have any doubts about the abilities of someone with mental illness, don't. Instead, be their support person.

Personally, pursuing my dreams with grit and determination was the one thing that gave me the skills to get me through life. My passion for filmmaking brought me to a healthy state of consciousness, which led me to a successful career. It became my catalyst for survival and a healthy identity to maintain. I came into my own when I embraced the music in my head and danced along.

Here's to my mom, and to having a glimpse of what it's like to be just like her. Here's to conquering mental illness and thriving, and to striving to solve bigger issues around wellness so everyone else can thrive too. Here's to overcoming the stigma and leading a healthy, balanced life.

About Holly Chadwick

Holly was raised by her grand-parents on Whidbey Island, who believed in rigorous music studies. Though she didn't become a concert pianist, she has directed short movies, documentaries, and now a web series called the *Sounds of Freedom*. She earned a B.A. in Film and Digital Media from the University of California, Santa Cruz and has studied fine art and digital media as far away as Italy and The Banff Centre in Alberta, Canada.

At the age of sixteen, Holly was a key member in a successful Internet start-up and went on to work for fine art and newspaper publishing companies in design and advertising, as well as in a darkroom developing crime scene photos.

Holly's father, who suffered with Post-Traumatic Stress Disorder, was the inspiration for *Sounds of Freedom*. She is also working on a documentary featuring her mother, mental illness, and herself called *Music in My Head*.

Holly resides on Whidbey Island in the same house she grew up in with her husband and two Golden Retrievers. She enjoys kayaking, boating, playing piano, extreme sledding and off-roading adventures. You can follow her projects at the following links:

eideticfilm.com
soundsoffreedomtheseries.com
musicinmyheadmovie.com (coming soon)
wellnesscreativemarketing.com
Facebook: facebook.com/soundsoffreedomtheseries/
Twitter: @freedom_of
Twitter: @holly_chadwick
Instagram: @hollyinaction
Instagram: @soundsoffreedomtheseries/

4

Starting Life Over

by Terry Jackson

Starting Life Over

Was it really twenty years ago that I stepped off the cliff, like the Fool of the Tarot's Major Archana? No net to catch me, no backup plan, no inkling of what was to come?

It all started with a ritual on New Year's Eve. I was ready to take another step in my spirituality, but I needed guidance. My best work comes from experiential training—show me and I'll get it, but give me a book and somehow I get totally confused. So, I prayed for a mentor, a teacher, prepared to do whatever I needed to do to find a closer relationship with the spirit world around me. I prayed, and then let it go—no thinking about it, just waiting for something to happen.

As the months rolled by, I took the advice of a good friend and decided to try and find my birth mom. Not knowing my heritage or ancestry left me asking questions about her. Where was she born? Why did she put me up for adoption? Are there any medical issues I need to know about? With my friend egging me on, I set out on a journey of discovery.

Being adopted and an only child leaves its mark in unusual ways. My memories of growing up are sparse, because without siblings there was no way to mark my journey through childhood. Siblings recount escapades, secrets, arguments, and encounters of many kinds, stimulating your memory, but as an only child I had no help in marking eventful situations. Despite my lack of siblings, though, my childhood was carefree and filled with adventure. What little kid gets to travel across the Atlantic Ocean to Naples, Italy on the USS Independence and return on the sister ship, the USS Constitution? I shudder sometimes when I look back and realize how spoiled I was. At least I behaved and had manners; being the daughter of an officer in the Air Force, I quickly learned to be polite.

I was very fortunate that my adoptive parents loved me and were able to provide a great life for me, but inside my heart I still longed to know where I came from. Why did I have certain likes and dislikes? Why did I love horses so much? Did I have any sisters or brothers?

While I was awaiting news about my birth mom, I took advantage of my eldest daughter's flight passes. Lucky me to have a daughter who is a flight attendant! I flew to Santa Cruz, California to attend a weekend spiritual seminar in the forests around the city. Because I was flying and had no idea what was going to be available around the campsite for meals, I brought power bars as well as a bag of colored pencils. I have an obsession with colored pens and pencils; they are almost more important to me than food. When I arrived, I found a beautiful campsite surrounded by tall firs with a fire pit in the middle of the circle. My friends helped me put up my tent and then took me down to the campground store for a meet-and-greet with the facilitator and the other participants. We sat around for what seemed like an eternity before Julia, our facilitator, showed up. Julia introduced me to a Chumash Indian named Sunman and asked him to take care of me. He had a car and the campsite was a long walk away from the camp store, so I was grateful for his help—especially since I had no idea where I was or how to get back to my tent!

Just as the meeting was about to end, I saw my caretaker walking away from me. I ran up to him, grabbed his arm, and said, "Hey, don't leave me! You are now my best friend." He laughed and told me he was just going to move all his stuff out of the passenger seat so I could sit down. Oh, good. I still kept him in my sight in case he decided to bolt.

Sunman took me back to the campsite and proceeded to unload his car. He had brought a camp stove, pots, pans, cooking utensils, propane, a coffee pot, and food. I offered him my power bars, and he just laughed and said he was going to make frybread, beans, and cowboy coffee, a favorite meal of his people. Oh, okay, I'm game! I soon learned that frybread is fried dough. Yummy. If it was something I had known about before I met him, my diet would have been in deep trouble. We talked until about one in the morning. During our conversations, I told him I was married and had two daughters. He talked about spending time on his reservation with his grandmother and living as an urban Native in Los Angeles. It was a lovely evening shared by two strangers who the Universe had brought together.

The next morning, we drove to the area where the workshop was being held. Sunman was there to dedicate the grounds at Julia's request as his people had lived in this area before the Spanish invaded and set up the Mission system. Sunman left fairly early with the excuse he had schoolwork to finish, and I was sad to see him go as I enjoyed his company.

The workshop was a bit on the cosmic woo-woo side, but the weekend was a nice reprieve from my everyday life. I was working sixty hours a week, attending massage school, and living with a man who had a short fuse and a bad temperament, didn't like to work, thought all his bosses were stupid, and was always right even when he was wrong. He quit work whenever he felt like it but I just kept working, spending seventeen years by this point in the legal division of a large bank. I would come home after eight at night, go to bed at ten, be up at five-thirty, and be out the door by six-thirty in the morning. I wish I hadn't felt so obligated to stay with him just because he adopted my first born. I also wished I hadn't made a promise to myself to never divorce my husband, never get married if he died, and never to move to California—the dang thing was going to rip off from the states and float past Alaska, and there was no way I was going on that trip. So, life plodded along. My husband and I had little to do with each other, and my dull life would have the occasional sprinkle of glitter when I was in touch with Sunman. Whereas my husband didn't get my "deep" thoughts, Sunman understood them and offered sage advice.

The next month I received a phone call from a woman from the Children's Home in St. Petersburg, Florida, where my sealed records were stored. She advised me that they had found my mom and that she indeed was open to a relationship with me; if she hadn't been, then that would be the end of the story. I lost it and fell onto my knees, wailing—I was glad no one was in the house to witness this spectacle. My adopted parents had passed years before, and to find my birth mom and have her willing to see me was almost more than I could bear. My soul was full of hope, but I also felt anxious. What if they didn't like me? What if I was really different from them, and we didn't have anything in common? Deep inside, I knew I was different—I always had been—but I decided they would meet the real me. I wasn't going to make myself to look more conservative and Midwestern to please anyone.

I was given her address, and I sent my mom a long letter giving her some of my history and the reasons why I was looking for her. After receiving my letter, she called me and we talked for the first time. She kept that letter till the day she died, when my sisters gave it back to me.

I was so excited to tell my husband that I had found my birth mom and that we would now have a bigger family. Since his parents had disowned him when he married me, I hoped that my side of the family would be more open to including us in their lives. When I shared the news, I was so surprised and hurt when my husband badgered me about how I was going to ruin our lives by introducing more people into it. I couldn't understand why in the world he would want to destroy my happiness. He had a sister and a brother, so he had those sibling memories. They couldn't all be bad memories; there had to be some good ones they laughed about. Why would he deny me this opportunity?

The date was set for the visit and I bedecked myself with the silver jewelry I always wore. My jewelry was my shield, my protection from any negativity that came my way. I was comfortable with my long straight hair, my black clothing, and my jewelry, but I wondered what reaction they would have, if any. I didn't worry too much about it, though, because I thought I might as well know up front whether or not they were going to like me for who I am.

Because of the cost of airfare, my daughter put me on a standby flight to Dallas where I would change planes and make my way to Tulsa, Oklahoma, and then someone would have to make the two-hour drive to pick me up. On the day of the trip, I felt like I had a tornado of butterflies in my stomach. When I spoke with my mom on the phone, I had learned that I have a stepdad, two half-sisters, a half-brother, two nieces, two nephews, an uncle and aunt and their two grandchildren, all of whom had never known of my existence until a few weeks prior. I kept thinking about this meeting. Was I doing the right thing, or was I opening Pandora's box? What if I didn't like them? My husband had refused to come with me and tried to discourage me from meeting my birth family, but this was something I had longed for since I was five years old. No one was going to stop me.

My mom picked me up at the airport alone—she said she didn't want to make our meeting a big production—and two hours later we arrived at our destination in Chanute, Kansas.

I am sure my family was a bit disconcerted at first to see a forty-seven-year-old woman with long straight hair and six pounds of turquoise and sterling silver jewelry, but to my eyes they were a lovely-looking family from the Midwest. They were conservative and engaging, and the evening was wonderful. There were no hard questions and no one was squirming to get out of there. I felt accepted. I had hoped that they weren't ax murderers, and my youngest sister had hoped I wasn't a brilliant scientist—no worries there. My other sister, who always thought she was the oldest, said she wished she had known because then she wouldn't have felt that she had to be a role model all her life.

That night, they told me how the rest of the family learned about my existence. My mom hadn't told anyone except my stepdad that she had another child, a daughter, whom she had given up for adoption. My stepdad told me that as soon as Mom told him about me, he wanted the two of them to head to Florida and get me. It was too late by then, of course, but I loved him so much for that gesture. My mom and stepdad kept my birth a secret for forty-seven years until the day the private investigator from the Children's Home contacted Mom. I can't imagine how shocked they all were.

After this meeting, I was walking on air. I had gone from a family of four to a large, boisterous clan full of people whom I loved. My mom answered all of my questions, and I know now I am Native American and Welsh on her side. I know that not everyone who searches for their family is so lucky, which has made me grateful for every day they are in my life. Both sets of my parents have passed now, and I have memories with all of them.

I came back to North Carolina feeling all warm and fuzzy, but I couldn't share this experience with my husband as I knew he would say something to ruin it for me. Both my daughters were out of the house—my youngest was in college and my oldest was working—so I was alone with my thoughts, but I could hold them deep in my heart and relish that I wasn't alone any more.

During this time, Sunman and I were still emailing. He was so refreshing and supportive, a large contrast to my husband. As we continued to keep in touch, I began to wonder if he was the teacher I had prayed for on New Year's Eve ten months before. I did put it out there that it was time for me to do what I wanted, and that I was ready to go anywhere to find my spiritual path and touch the mysteries of the *Universe*. Could he be who I was looking for?

I didn't know how this was possible, especially since he wasn't what I had imagined. He was ten years younger than me and lived in Los Angeles, and as previously stated, I would never move to California due to the whole "floating off to Alaska" situation. I was also married and dedicated to making my relationship work, no matter what. I told Sunman that I was obligated to my husband because he married me even though his parents disowned him for it. I thought I made this clear to both of us. But as the weeks passed by, Sunman kept feeding me food for thought. He asked, how long will you be obligated? It's been twenty-three years. Another time he prompted, how much do you want what you say you need? I told him I'd have to get back to him in two or three days on that one. And then there was a kicker: if you weren't married, I'd marry you. And that was it.

With encouragement from him and from my massage therapy friends, I left my husband and boarded a runaway train to wonderland. I have no idea how I managed to leave because I'm a weenie and hate to hurt anyone's feelings. Liquor helped.

To make matters worse, the movers, who were supposed to come in the afternoon while my husband was at work, came at night instead. My husband sat on the porch, watching as a small portion of my personal belongings were loaded into a truck—I left most of the things we had accumulated over the years. It was awful. My stomach was spinning, and I felt like a traitor. But I didn't feel bad enough to stop. Sunman was staying nearby with a friend of mine, and he and my friend kept encouraging me over the phone. I walked out the door for the last time that night and drove away.

While this decision was tough in the moment, I don't feel guilty for leaving my husband. My daughters and family have helped me realize that I did what I had to do. They totally understood the reasons I left, and they are happy that I now have the life I always wanted.

Sunman and I drove from North Carolina to Los Angeles, stopping in Kansas to introduce him to my family. They loved him. My mom told me later that she was happy I left with Sunman—she had met my husband, and she wasn't a fan. It helped to know that my family believed I did the right thing.

Another stop was in Northern Arizona to meet Sunman's mom. He warned me when we first contemplated this coupling that his mother was difficult. I said it was no problem for me; I can handle difficult. Turns out that no, I can't, especially when the real definition of "difficult" is impossible. Boy, she didn't like me. I was older than her son and had fair skin, and she was sure I would try and take him away from her. She insulted me, yelled at me, played tricks on me, and criticized me, everything she could think of to make me leave. And she almost succeeded. There came a time when I told Sunman we couldn't do this anymore, as this constant battle was wearing us both down. He called his mother and told her I was leaving, and she in turn called me and told me not to. A brief truce was created, and although it didn't last long it gave me enough time to become determined to stick it out. I loved Sunman, so I wasn't going to let her get the best of me. My whole attitude was to be in grace—I never let her have an opportunity to say anything bad about me without having to lie. It was one of the hardest things I've ever done, but the thought of living the rest of my life without Sunman was intolerable.

Time always seems to make a difference in these matters, and it did with us. I gave Sunman and his mom plenty of time together without me; I had a new family I was anxious to be around, so these absences worked. It was hard, but it was well worth it. Twenty years later we are in a wonderful place in our relationship and his mom has come around to even like me, I think. Life is not easy, even when you think it's going to be, but when you want something so much it becomes easier to stand strong and to do what you have to do to make things work.

Sunman's "hovel" as he called it was in the Crenshaw area. He was so worried that I was not going to be happy living here, especially since his duplex was so much smaller than the house I had lived in. But, you can make any house a home. Our bedroom was one-quarter of a larger room, with just enough space for a full bed and a small side table. An entertainment center divided this space from the other side of the room, which contained what was left over from his ceramic business. But none of that mattered. I even endured visits from his mom, which always filled me with anxiousness, but I survived and learned ways to deflect her criticism.

Sunman danced in pow wows when he was young but had stopped when he and his mother went into the ceramic business. A few years before we met, he had put new regalia together and started dancing again as a Southern Straight dancer, which is one of the traditional dances for men. I went with him to several pow wows—I knew nothing about it at first, but I learned fast. His mother lent me a shawl so I could dance intertribal, where spectators are welcome into the arena. At one dance, as he was dressing with his mother's help, she handed over the honor of being the one to help dress him. She told me if anything fell off him she would kill me dead, and I believed her. If anything falls of the dancer when they are dancing, he/she must pick up the item and leave the arena. I wasn't sure I was happy with this honor; in fact, it scared me to death. Luckily his regalia is now easy for him to put on himself; I'm the one who needs help!

While we were still in Los Angeles, a friend and principal chief of a tribe in the east called and asked if we would meet her in California at a Fasting Camp. Dorothy had been invited by a Shawnee man, Jesse, who ran a week-long encampment that he had been facilitating for around twenty-five years. She also told us that his uncle, Bearheart, was going to be there. Bearheart was a Muskogee/Creek Medicine Man whose book, *The Wind is My Mother*, I had read years before. We had an engagement during that time and couldn't attend the full week, but we both agreed that we had to go.

Sunman and I were both totally clueless as to what "fasting camp" was. We soon learned it was what we referred to as a Vision Quest, where people were put on a mountain or in the forest in a sacred circle to fast for a number of days. Jesse's way was to put up fasters with their pipe, or with a borrowed one they could use for four years. These fasters were then recognized as pipe carriers, or culture carriers, by other Native people and others who were familiar with the Indigenous culture of the United States. However, on that visit we were part of the spectators who stayed in camp. We would sit around after dinner and Jesse would tell stories. Over the past twenty years I've heard most of the stories over and over, but there is always some nugget of knowledge that someone needs to hear.

The first ceremony of the camp was an opening pipe ceremony. I had no idea I was supposed to bring a shawl—I didn't even know there would be a pipe ceremony during camp. Another lesson: if there is a sacred pipe involved, women always wear a shawl and skirt out of respect. Jesse gave me a small shawl to wrap around my waist. Walking around the grounds, we were stopped by an unhappy woman who aggressively asked why I was wearing that shawl. I was startled and told her that Jesse and his wife, Rae, told me to wear it. This was a taste of what was to come for me in my quest for my Native identity. Thankfully she backed off after hearing my explanation, and we since have become sisters/friends.

Although Sunman and I stayed for only three days, we were able to experience a sweat lodge. Sunman attended sweat lodges at his reservation when he was younger, but this was my first time. The sweat lodges were for purification of the fasters and of those who would stay in camp as supporters and feast on their behalf. The fasters would be put in a sacred circle in the woods with their pipe, praying for the people. The men would have no water or food while the women would be given a small bottle of water, just in case.

While the fasters were fasting, the rest of us hung around camp or went swimming in the creek. Sunman and I had such a wonderful time. The mountains, the forest, and the creek made me feel at home; it was the most beautiful place I had ever seen. We met a lot of people, and Sunman actually reconnected with a childhood friend. I was sorry we had to leave early, but we promised to return for the next ceremony. We asked our hosts to give us a call if any property came up for sale, as I was ready to beg, borrow or steal to get a piece of land there. I'm sure they looked at me as a white woman, but I did my best to look like I knew what I was doing, especially after the shawl episode.

Before the next ceremony, a piece of land was put on the market and Jesse called to ask if we were interested. We immediately took out a home equity loan and bought the property right next to the ceremonial grounds. This move started a long and deep friendship between the four of us.

By the winter ceremony I was ready to make a pledge to fast. Pledges at this camp entailed a commitment to fast during the week-long camp every year for four years. How many days you fast is up to your mentor—no one knows how many days and nights of your life you'll be spending in a circle praying for the people. To Sunman and Jesse it was probably way too early for someone who didn't grow up Native to take on such a sacred pledge, but to me I was making up on lost time. My pledge was accepted and I fasted the next summer, and I have continued to fast every year for the past sixteen years.

Four years after we first started attending the fasting camp, I was visiting Jesse and Rae when without notice Jesse said we were going to town to the fabric store. Okay, fine. Both of them were pow wow dancers, so I figured that somebody must need a new outfit. Walking around the store, Jesse started showing me some cotton calico material. Do you like this one? How about this one? I wondered why he was asking me. I commented that I really like the red one, but what does Rae think? It's for her, right? Nope. It was for me.

I was told I was going to dance, and I was stunned. I loved pow wows, but I was only ever a spectator. Dance? In front of all those Natives who would be judging me? I wasn't sure I wanted to take this on, but in this culture when an elder or mentor tells you to do something, you have no choice but to do it. I gulped and said sure.

Getting ready to dance can take years; you need outfits, bead work, moccasins, a feather fan, a belt, the list goes on and on. Either you make these things yourself, or your family helps. The woman who asked me about my shawl that first time at fasting camp made me some dresses, taught me how to bead, and made me moccasins. Rae taught me how to dance southern style—the style of dance she, Jesse, and Sunman danced. She made me go around and around her living room to pow wow songs so I would learn how to dance correctly. These lessons made me so nervous; she had been a professional dancer and was now a choreographer, and I had two left feet.

Sunman had me listen to southern style pow wow songs so I would learn when to stop at the end, how to dance on beat, and how to know when to bend down at the honor beats. It was grueling. And to make it more stressful, I had to have a "coming out." This is a new pow wow dancer's introduction to the arena, a time for family and friends to witness your entry into the pow wow circle. It is protocol to have a coming out; to have someone speak for you to give highlights of your life, and for the new dancer to thank people who helped him or her get ready with gifts, usually a small token to say thank you.

My coming out was held in a park where friends and family gathered to witness my first dance. My Navajo sister/friend, Chucki, shared this coming out with me. Sunman took Chucki and me out in front of everyone to introduce us and to talk about our accomplishments and who we were in the Native community. A friend who was head singer for a southern drum group composed a song for me, and he and the other singers sang this song while Chucki and I danced in a circle. When the song was over, we had our small giveaway. Sunman provided food for the occasion, and we all sat around talking, joking and having a grand time. It was quite wonderful.

Today I'm more comfortable dancing at pow wows because Sunman and I have a lot of friends with whom we pow wow, and I know they have my back. I've had experiences where Native women have refused to shake my hand or ignored me, and I'm sure things are said about me behind my back, but that's okay. I'm doing what I love. I'm accepted by a group of Natives who see beyond the fair skin and see me as an Indigenous woman. For those who are less accepting, I know and follow the protocol and have answers ready if someone comes and asks who gave me permission to dance. I have fasted for sixteen years and will be going for my seventeenth year next summer when I'm seventy. I am a pipe carrier and a culture carrier. I earned the right to carry a pipe, and yet my pipe is a personal pipe I use to pray for people. I have not been given an altar, with the right to conduct ceremonies; I didn't grow up Native and don't have the knowledge of those who did. I don't take my pipe out in the community and conduct pipe ceremonies because I don't have the right to do so, and that's okay. It is as it should be. What I do experience on a day-to-day basis is enough for me.

I don't need to, nor should I want to, go around saying I'm a Medicine Woman. I'm not. My job, as I see it, is to be a role model. I spent twenty years learning these Native ways. As my mentor would say, I've come a long way, but I have a long way to go. And that's perfect. I am in this for the long haul. I don't need to prove anything to anyone; I know who I am now. I am comfortable in my skin. I hold my spirituality to my chest and embrace it. I love my new life, and I will never do anything to jeopardize it.

Throughout my epic journey there were many twists and turns, roadblocks to negotiate, and big girl panties to pull up, but I would do it again in a heartbeat. Finding my family was life-changing, and my time with my mom was profound. Her greatest gift to me was her acceptance and introduction to the rest of her, and now my, family. Meeting Sunman and making the choice to leave my husband and create a new life with him was the best decision I've ever made. Sure, we've had difficult obstacles to surmount, but we have the strength and love to meet anything head on. We will continue to live a traditional life, keeping our commitment to and being a resource for the community. I look forward to seeing where this journey takes me next.

About Terry Jackson

Terry Jackson is a traditional Native grandmother who has fostered her spirituality and creativity throughout her life. She celebrates the sacredness of the feminine and shares her story to encourage women on their journey through life. As a global wanderer who has traveled to Machu Picchu, Egypt, Dubai, Europe, and other places near and far, Terry is an experiential learner whose life lessons have come from a variety of experiences, including being adopted and finding her birth family.

Terry is also a certified massage therapist, aromatherapist, and hypnotherapist. She enjoys creating jewelry, writing, beading items for her pow wow regalia, and making lotions and potions utilizing her knowledge of essential oils.

She and her husband opened the only Native-owned trading post in Tucson, Arizona in 2005. Their first inventory included many pieces from their own collection, and they now have a well-stocked trading post with something for everyone. It is an anchor in the Tucson community and enjoys solid relationships with the University of Arizona, the American Indian Law School Students Association, the Tucson Indian Center, the VA Hospital, and more.

www.sacredgroundstp.com
Email: azontheroadagain@gmail.com
Facebook: Terry Davidson Jackson
Facebook: Sacred Grounds Trading Post
Instagram: @azshawnee
Twitter: @ChiMouse49

5

Giving Ourselves the Space
to Lead

by Jane Beausire

Giving Ourselves the Space
to Lead

As a child, I loved being. I loved exploring and spent many hours in the Mexican countryside, where I grew up conquering rocks that were kingdoms, making pots out of mud, and generally enjoying the freedom to discover my interests in a safe and loving environment. I loved the Mexican culture—the colors, the smells, the energy of the market, and the kindness of the people who would invite me to share tortillas cooked fresh on open fires. I loved being in touch with what was essential, and I believed that everything was possible. It sounds like a fairy tale now, but from my perspective as a young girl filled with imagination and a fierce love of life and discovery, it was very real. In retrospect, what I really treasure about this time of my life was being totally unconscious to any need for acknowledgment from others—I just was. As expats in Mexico, I was nurtured by the love and presence of our extended family of friends, and especially by the Mexican maids who were in many ways my primary caregivers.

With time and life experiences, including moving with my family to New Zealand when I was nine, this freedom and connection to myself, to life, and to my own deepest potential became more and more tenuous. On the outside I seemed brave and faced the challenges of such a radical shift without hesitation, but on the inside I was shaken up and desperately looking for any form of anchor or familiar rock on which to build my foundations. I missed Mexico desperately. Our family was proud of our heritage—I was born in Mexico to a father who had been brought up in Chili, Switzerland, and UK and a mother who was born in New Zealand and travelled to Peru—but having such a diverse background wasn't considered "normal" in New Zealand society in the '70s. My sense of not belonging and of having no roots or familiar childhood bonds led to a deep sense of disconnection, and I began to focus on getting approval and a sense of foundation from the outside world rather than the inside.

This need to be noticed by others flourished once I was old enough to go to high school as I discovered that I could anchor my sense of self on my success in different activities and classes. I threw myself into music, acting, and every possible sport while also keeping focused on my grades. I was a good all-rounder—there was nothing I was particularly spectacular at, but I was recognized for the efforts that I made. I drove myself unbelievably hard, finding enjoyment in having a sense of purpose. What I didn't realize was that this focus on perfection was a cover-up for a deep-seated sense of inadequacy.

In my final year of school, I developed anorexia as another way of calling out to be noticed whilst at the same time wanting to disappear, or possibly as a result of my fear of taking up too much space. As with the rest of my life, I took my anorexia as an opportunity to demonstrate that I was strong and capable and able to defeat it despite the odds. I was the one who took my mother to the doctor when my form teacher shared that they were worried about me. I've never forgotten the tears and the victory of the first spoonful of soup that was to begin the long journey back to health. This constant paradox between "I want to take my place and demonstrate that I am okay" and "I take up too much space, who am I to dare to take my place in this world" is a theme that weaved its way into my life and created a soul-destroying level of distress and confusion.

After having gained enough weight to pass as "normal," I put on a brave face and set out to conquer life. I took a year off before starting university and travelled to France, where I became an au pair for a Parisian family. I survived the trip, but in many ways it was a year of isolation and loneliness as I struggled to find sense in the world around me and to reconnect to something that would provide me with solace and guidance. I was so excited to be in Paris, but the reality of being so alone amongst so many people was excruciating. The French culture (and specifically the Parisian culture) can be quite hard to integrate into. I was treated quite badly by my host family, who forced me to live away from them and do housework rather than caring for the kids. In retrospect, I was also very vulnerable as I was still recovering from anorexia. I was determined to make this work though and refused to give up, although I was likely motivated by wanting to make my parents proud rather than pursuing my own personal growth and fulfillment.

Once I returned to New Zealand, I set off to university with a dream of attending medical school to become a doctor. My grades were just short of being admitted directly, so in my entrance year I needed to earn a place in the program. I had actually wanted to be a nurse, but my parents were unsupportive. My mother in particular was totally against this plan—in her generation women were only allowed to be nurses or teachers, and she wanted me to take advantage of the opportunities that women were now being offered. So, I upgraded my dream. At the same time, my school, my teachers, and my parents all thought that I wouldn't make the grade I needed to be accepted into medicine. In retrospect, I think they were worried about the pressure I would face when travelling this path, but I took their concern to mean that I would not be good enough, and this just made me more determined.

At university I again struggled with being the odd one out as it wasn't that common for people to take a year off before starting. I also believe that whilst I had recovered from anorexia on the outside, I had never dealt with the fundamental causes and dis-ease from which I was suffering. Within a few months my body began to rebel and I had to have major abdominal surgery, which meant I missed a significant number of school weeks and was going to lose my opportunity to go to med school. This fed the voice that was telling me I was no good. It was like an internal war, with one part of me saying "you can do and be anything you want" and another part saying "you can't be a doctor, you'll never make the grade." I quickly descended into a deep depression which led to me being hospitalized and having to leave school. It was a raw and difficult time where I was called to explore the darkest side of human nature, but it was also a time where I was sensitive and overwhelmed by the beauty and warmth of some of the simplest gestures and connections. I could no longer build myself up based on a persona defined by the outside world, and I needed to dig deep into my beliefs to find sense within the suffering. To do this, I had to reconnect with my soul and my body and begin to explore and connect with what really mattered to me. I also needed to acknowledge and speak about a trauma that I had experienced years ago, just before leaving Mexico.

One sunny day when I was eight years old, I wandered down the road from our house in Mexico City alone, something I was forbidden to do. There were some stables that I loved to visit because I enjoyed seeing the horses that lived there. Usually I went with our maid, but today I was by myself. When I arrived, I was welcomed by someone I had seen there before. He asked me if I wanted to visit the boxes where the horses were kept overnight. I hesitated at first, but I sort of knew him and he seemed like a kind man. Once we were inside, he started behaving strangely and inappropriately, but I was a terrified young girl who wasn't supposed to be there and I was totally unable to defend myself. In that moment I just wanted to survive, and so I completely switched off and disappeared elsewhere. When he had finished, he held me close and whispered in my ear that if I ever told anybody what had occurred he would make something very, very bad happen to my father and to our family. I returned home feeling as though I was in a dream. I was terrified that someone would find out and the man would come after my family, so I never told anyone what happened. I remember becoming a bit withdrawn and wetting my bed, but otherwise I just seemed to be able to go on. However, a few months later my father was defrauded in a business investment, and we had to sell our property in Mexico to move to New Zealand with all of the loss and sadness this entailed. In my innocent eight-year-old mind, I thought that I was the cause of all this loss—that somehow I had let everyone down that day in the stable.

It was a hard journey to share but speaking about it to the team looking after me in the hospital, as well as to the other patients, gave me the chance to finally cry from the depths of my soul, releasing the pain and anger I felt for the loss of the beautiful innocent child I had been. Above all, I needed to find my voice to whisper, to say, to shout, to scream "IT WAS NOT MY FAULT," and then to actually believe those five powerful and precious words, little by little. This marked the beginning of the next phase of my life where I would gently, slowly, and deliberately step into each experience, taking my courage with both hands and embracing the opportunities that life was generously presenting me.

After being in and out of the hospital for several years, I eased myself into a full-time job as a receptionist. I returned to sports and reconnected with the strength and beauty of my body. I delighted in the friends and the social circle I joined—dancing, hiking, swimming naked at midnight and then getting caught dripping wet in knickers, bra, and socks by a police patrol—as well as in my first true love affair and the joyful liberation I felt as a young woman coming into bloom. Every moment was precious and nothing was taken for granted as I gained this deep-seated respect for life, and for the second chance I was being given.

At twenty-five, I woke at one in the morning and knew that the time had come for me to return to university. I no longer felt a desire to go to medical school after beginning my own healing journey, and I was also aware that there were other skills and abilities that I wanted to develop by going to business school—I was ready, and I was being called. What an amazing adventure this was, although one that was not easy at first as university came with memories of failure. The reminder notice I received before my year one final exams telling me that the university would not accept me back if I failed also wasn't very reassuring. Thankfully, I worked really hard and loved what I was doing, so I excelled. I discovered my curiosity to learn as well as an intelligence that I had never been able to channel before. I continued to grow and enjoy my social life, but I was also able to listen to my needs on a deeper level.

In the last year of my four-year program, I acknowledged that I was still being held back by my experience in Mexico and that I needed to take my healing one step further. I requested a three-month sabbatical, which the school was not very comfortable with and would also mean that I would not graduate with my friends. However, I knew deep down that this was an essential step for me so I took this precious time. I found the funds to book myself into a private clinic, and with the strength and power that I now knew I had as a twenty-eight-year-old woman, I went back to do the deep work I needed to do so I could be free to take flight on the next stage of my life's journey. Inspired by my connection to my deep feminine energy, along with the wisdom from books such as Clarissa Pinkola Estés' *Women Who Run With the Wolves* and a beautiful therapist I had been working with, I stood my ground and faced my story once again. I confronted and fought the dragons that were still weighing me down with the love and support of an environment where I could be as vulnerable and safe as I needed in that moment. It was the last time I would be in a clinical environment, and I was proud to be there by choice and to have had the courage to acknowledge that I needed the help. It was a gift I gave to myself. My healing journey still continues to this day, and while it takes other forms now, it is still an integral part of me. Rather than seeing this event as something I need to hide or get over, I know that it is just one strand of the tapestry that makes me who I am.

At this time, I also felt courageous enough to share what had happened with my parents, something I had not done before now. They had always kept me and my "illness" at arm's length, loving me ferociously but not knowing how to be there for me. Telling them about what happened was a profound moment, and I am deeply grateful to have been able to share this with them. I told them at separate moments, starting with my mother. She was deeply moved, and she shared that she had wondered if something had happened but didn't know how to ask. My father had more difficulty understanding or even hearing what I said, but I know that it was very distressing for him as a father not to have been able to protect me. It is true that I have felt angry that they never noticed my distress as a child, but being able to share the truth now allowed us to build a new way of being with each other, surrounded by the love and respect we all shared.

Once I returned to university for the final few months of my program, I was invited to apply for a scholarship for a prestigious business school in Paris. A part of me wanted to unfold my wings and fly whilst another part wanted to stay and enjoy the learning I had achieved. I struggled between wanting to reconnect with the cosmopolitan energy I had known and loved in Mexico, my desire to go back to France and make it work this time, and wanting to enjoy the serenity, peace, and nature of my life in New Zealand. As was often the case, I went deep inside and I asked my intuition what I should do. I realized that I wanted to at least apply for the scholarship, and then the response would make the decision for me. I applied and won the scholarship, so a few months short of my thirtieth birthday I left New Zealand—the land that I had come to love, and which had healed and held me through my biggest life transition—to go to Europe and explore the opportunities it held. I knew intuitively that I was not likely to return to New Zealand after my schooling had finished as the market there was fairly limited; it was quite likely that I would be making my next home in Europe. The move was challenging—as much as I love change, I find it to be very unsettling and destabilizing when it happens. My foundations were still rather fragile as well, so I was more susceptible to being shaken up. I also discovered that I was the eldest student in the program and was better suited to the MBA stream, but it was not possible for me to make the change.

On one particularly difficult and wet day, I prayed to my spiritual guides and asked, "Please give me a sign that I'm in the right place at the right time, or I'm leaving!" My journey has often been guided by my intuition but also by a strong spiritual connection that I have felt since my early childhood in Tepotzlan, one which I have developed throughout my healing journey. In addition to being brought up as a Christian and really confronting what this means for me, I have been deeply influenced by Buddhist philosophy, yoga, and the wisdom of different sacred and spiritual practices worldwide. After this prayer I went down to the local village for some groceries, and when I returned there was a letter waiting for me stating that I had won a second scholarship to support my studies in France from a Women's Federation in New Zealand. I grimaced at first, and then I smiled because I knew my answer. However tough it was going to be, I was in the right place.

My studies went well, and I particularly enjoyed doing an exchange semester at the Stockholm School of Economics. I found the culture to be similar to New Zealand, and the students I was studying with were more diverse and of a similar age and background to myself. It was here that I had my first glimpse of what would become my guiding interest in business: leadership development. We were learning about organizational development, cross-culture, and leadership, and I loved the focus on the human side of business as well as the intercultural perspectives. We had one particular professor from Ireland who opened my eyes and my heart to explore different perspectives on culture and the people side of business—he was a Gestalt therapist who created a safe space for us to explore our fundamental beliefs and values. It was so interesting to be able to articulate the influence of culture on the way we behave as individuals, but also as groups and communities. This experience also allowed me to understand the challenges and conflicts I had faced as the child of someone who came from a different culture, as well as the processes I experienced in shifting from one country to another. Without realizing it, I was stepping onto a pathway that would become my career.

When I finished my master's degree with a plan to work in marketing, life intervened once again and took me down an unexpected path. I came out of a series of interviews for a large pharma firm with both good news and bad. The bad was that I was too experienced for their graduate marketing program, but the good news was that I was offered a role in strategic human resources. When life comes calling, I step into it, and so off I went with no regrets.

The start of this new career was intense and satisfying, with amazing opportunities for growth, travel, and discovery. I had a level of financial security that I had never known, being able to repay the debts I had from my years of study. I explored the different career opportunities that were offered to me, although it wasn't always easy as I had to navigate and learn about power, politics, and business in the corporate world. A role in the UK was followed by another one in Switzerland and then a return to France. Through these different transitions, I was challenged as a person to make choices that were often counter-intuitive to common business and career practices as well as to adapt culturally to new countries and environments. I chose to go deeper into roles that involved helping people realize their potential and continued to explore my own personal and spiritual development as I wove together my interests in business, psychology, culture, and wellbeing. It was essential for me to explore and learn how to navigate through the different experiences I was living whilst also searching for a profound sense of purpose, sacredness, and connection to life. I had a deep need to find the meaning of my journey as part of my ongoing healing process, so I read many books on psychology, philosophy, spirituality, and health as well as developing a practice of yoga and meditation. I also returned to therapy and trained as a career counsellor, a Gestalt practitioner, and eventually as an executive coach. I challenged myself to consider whether I truly wanted to continue working in the corporate world, but I felt intuitively that this was where I wanted to be. I was forging my own career path, one that was certainly a little different, but I trusted my intuition and my own North Star.

At the same time, my career journey was also entwined with my life choices and the growth I experienced through love, life, and loss. I met and fell in love with my husband at the business school in France. He was funny, intelligent, and cultivated. In retrospect, I believe we both fell in love with what the other represented—stability and a deep sense of belonging from him and an open, pioneering, and exotic international background from me. We were very different but shared the same desire to create a loving home. I decided to return to France to join him, and although we had some challenges getting pregnant we were blessed with a son in 2005. We loved being young parents and gave ourselves heart and soul to this new role, *although there were certainly challenges*. I struggled with the loneliness of having a baby in another country and I missed my parents terribly. I was also questioning my relationship as there was a level of intimacy and care that was missing, and it was hard to know if it was part of my own personal difficulties, if it was cultural, or if there truly was a lack of love. My investment in my career and my personal development was in part to answer these questions, and also partly to pretend to the outside world that all was well. It seemed as though we were doing everything we could to create happiness, but the results didn't feel real and robust.

My mother was diagnosed with cancer when my son was three, and within eighteen months she had left us. It was incredibly difficult being so far away—although my beloved brother and I were very involved every step of the way, the distance made it unbelievably hard and trips to be with her meant I had to leave my young son behind. I had support from my family in France, but leaving without him was always heart-wrenching. I did however have the gift of being able to accompany my mother as she passed, and this experience gave me the opportunity to understand the importance of life and to challenge my own desires and reality.

At this time, I was also a full-time HR leader within a mid-sized hi-tech company. It was a challenging position as I was the only woman and only non-French person on a leadership team that was driving the business through a significant organizational transition. I had to learn that while I could no longer be liked, I could be respected. I made mistakes, but I also grew and helped the organization attain a new level of strength and vision. It was an experience that was rich in learning and deepened my insights into leadership development and the operational challenges of driving transformation and growth.

Over the next few years, I realized that I wanted to fly free and become a freelance coach and trainer specializing in leadership and management development. At the same time, I wanted to explore the challenge of how to work in a way that would nourish me and allow me to be more present and authentic, both in my career and in my private life. I was trying desperately to make my marriage work as well as accompanying my father on his last journey, but it became increasingly clear that I needed to let go and just accept that nothing I could do was going to change either situation. I needed to return to that place of deep trust that I had known before.

To experience so much loss in such a short time was profoundly moving and started the next stage of my journey, a journey that I am still navigating several years later. It's been a call to return to what is essential once again, and in my vulnerability I have been reminded not only of the strength I have, but also of my need to have the resources to continue forward with courage and serenity.

My choice to let go, move on, take risks, and trust myself has been such an opportunity. I am growing in ways I could never have imagined, and I have found hidden resources both within myself and within others. I have become more fragile and more real. I know that every day and every situation is not only made up of circumstances, but more importantly with what we think and what we say to ourselves about those circumstances. When things get really tough, we can either go down the familiar rabbit holes that our egos and our minds naturally follow, or we can observe our thoughts, take a step back, breathe, and choose where we go next. It is this focus that invites us to reconnect with what matters most and to make those choices more consciously for ourselves, for the people around us, for the organizations we care about, and for the planet as a whole.

I'm still very much on this journey, but what life has given me is the opportunity to learn and practice focusing inward as well as outward to create a very powerful tool for change. My focus in my work has been on organizational leaders, but I prefer to acknowledge leaders as all those who seek to guide others towards any form of change or transformation—it doesn't have to be role-related. We can be a leader in the way we turn up and inspire others. We can be a leader in the way we lean into change and courageously own the challenges we will face if we want to move forwards. We can be a leader by creating conditions for new ideas, new practices, and new processes to emerge and take form. I used to believe that I couldn't work in the field of leadership development since I had never held a high-level job in a Fortune 500 company, but now I know that my own journey has provided me with a depth of understanding of what I believe leadership is about as we move through complex and challenging times.

Over the last few years, my spiritual growth has deepened with learning from Buddhist teachings in authentic leadership as well as from two deeply inspiring teachers who have guided me away from a focus on *doing* to a focus on *being*. They have challenged me, encouraged me, inspired me, and taught me about our place in the world, our connection with the earth, our responsibility to step up on behalf of our children, the power of returning to our true values, the wisdom of the elders, and the power of forgiveness. It's a path that doesn't preach dogma but instead provides insight and tools that allow us to seek and find what is sacred and essential in our day-to-day lives, wherever we are and whatever we are doing.

My deepest belief is that it is time to allow leadership to be encouraged at every level of our communities so that each and every one of us can participate in facilitating transformation and change. I believe that so much of what every person brings to the table is their own life journey and experiences—there is such power and insight available to us if only we would give ourselves permission to share and to listen. I also believe that many of us need to step up and dare to do what we are being called to do. The stakes are high, and if we simply hide in the background then we are depriving the world of the solutions and gifts that are the reason we are here. We need to listen to the wisdom of the elders and to those who come from cultures where they are more connected to what is essential and less dispersed by modern thought and consumerism. I also believe that those of us who have more experience in life should facilitate opportunities for the upcoming generations to step up and share their perspectives, their ideas, and their leadership, and then we should get out of their way. I believe that the next generation has a way of thinking and a freshness that will help us find solutions that are more relevant to the challenges we face today.

I hope that my experience and journey is an invitation for you to honor your own journey and your own calling to take care of yourself, and to know that both are at the heart of all transformation. In those moments where you question why you are here, stay still and listen to your heart, feel the wind and the ground beneath your feet, and trust that you know what to do. Just place one foot in front of the other, breathe, and simply be the wonderful, beautiful soul that you are.

About Jane Beausire

Jane Beausire is a learning and development professional, an executive coach, and a speaker with a special focus on meaningful and mindful leadership for women, young leaders, and those interested in exploring how we can return to what matters in the way we live, lead, and care for ourselves and the communities around us.

She has been on her own spiritual and growth journey from a very young age and is inspired by the wisdom of the different elders and cultures that are calling us to transform and change the way we lead in the world. She has lived in six different countries as well having had the honor of accompanying clients from Africa, Asia, the Americas, Oceania, and Europe. Through this experience, she has observed the power of what we can achieve if we collaborate across borders—heart to heart, hand in hand, and heads together.

She is very excited to share and to see how she can be of service to the Wild and Wise Women community.

www.aio-resources.com
Email: info@aio-resources.com
LinkedIn: Jane Beausire

6

Creating Balance Through Self-Respect

by Sue Bonzell

Creating Balance Through Self-Respect

Respect. It's something everyone will tell you is vital in our lives. Respect is the model of kindness, consideration, and tolerance that is important in personal relationships, and most importantly in our relationship with ourselves. Respect is recognizing that we are all human, regardless of our flaws, our poor judgment, our lineage, or our life circumstances. It is offering tolerance for those who are not like us, which can often be difficult to do. It is acknowledging people for who they are, adhering to the rules that help keep our society from devolving into utter chaos, and showing courtesy and consideration to others for no other reason than recognizing that they are who they are. It is looking up to and admiring people who do amazing things and offering tribute to those who complete a job well done, and most importantly to ourselves.

To me, respect is the foundation of everything—every relationship, every human interaction, every communication, and everything we touch in this world. I see respect as the umbrella policy for integrity, trust, gratitude, and love. All of those things cannot exist without a foundation of respect.

I was not aware of this understanding until I embarked on a journey of self-discovery, which many of us often do as we age gracefully. I had hired a life coach in an effort to jump-start my transformational journey—of course, I didn't know it was a transformational journey at the time! During our sessions, we talked over and over about things that severely triggered me and sent me into an angry or fearful state. I was frustrated that these occurrences were so frequent, and that some very simple events would bring out the worst in me and cause me to become ridiculously upset. Journaling became a way of life—as I experienced these triggering situations, I started to write them down so I could track my negative reactions. And let me tell you, I now have a small library of overstuffed journals filled with as much drivel as there is revelation. After months of frustration and endless hours of journaling, I finally saw it: a pattern. Every single thing that had triggered me basically boiled down to one thing, and that one single thing was respect—or a lack of it, to be more precise.

Upon further inspecting this huge, life-changing discovery, I was encouraged to look back at my childhood to see what experiences may have led me to be so triggered by a lack of respect. In the process, I began to see my childhood a bit differently. I was able to recognize and appreciate that my upbringing taught me many lessons and ultimately has shown me the path to where I am now, and for that I am grateful.

I have spoken to many people who have had experiences that are similar to mine, growing up with fathers who had a drinking problem and left their kids and wives at home to spend most nights at the bars. My father was a narcissist, only engaging or caring when things revolved around him, and arriving home drunk was standard practice. I can remember coming home with my mom and sister late one night after a movie to find that the front door was left wide open. My dad's keys were on the floor of the entry hall, and after venturing into the house we discovered my dad passed out on the bathroom floor. I remember asking my mom if he was dead.

My father had very little input in the parenting of me and my sister. That burden lay entirely upon my mother's shoulders, who not only had to parent us kids but also my father. My mother was the perfect co-dependent and a great enabler, remaining in a loveless marriage for fifty-two years. They finally divorced when they were in their seventies. My mom said she stayed "because of the kids," which to me made no sense at all. Their dysfunctional relationship only served to display to their children what hatred, disrespect, and verbal abuse looked like. The real reason she stayed was that in all of her strength and independence, she lacked the confidence that she could go it on her own and still survive. Fear was holding her in a place where she could never thrive. She lacked the self-respect that would have helped her set boundaries with my father and trust in herself. She rarely took care of herself and was truly unaware of the power she possessed.

I had admired my mother's strength to persevere through financial troubles, verbal abuse, and unending stress, although this created an overworked, underappreciated, and sometimes bitter mom. In an attempt to finally better her life and not depend solely on my father for income, she became a Realtor when she was forty-seven. This was a path I would myself follow at the age of forty-five as a broke, single woman. She became my mentor and I became her best friend—the only person she confided in or showed raw authenticity and vulnerability to.

As an adult, I had no idea how well-versed I had become in disrespect until I was getting divorced for the second time and my then-husband proclaimed that I had been borderline verbally abusive to him. That was a gut punch and a big wake-up call for me.

As my transformative journey progressed, I realized that if I were to loudly proclaim that respect was my number one core value, then I had to examine how respectfully I was showing up in my life on a regular basis. This was an exercise that would push me to write a book called *The Respect Experiment*. It was an examination and unfolding of the role of respect in my life, and my "aha" moment was the largest chapter in the book—the one on self-respect.

While writing the book, I asked myself, "How am I showing respect to myself?" I lacked solid boundaries, and when I did have them I rarely stuck to them. I was constantly talking down to myself, which is also known as negative self-talk, and I wasn't as confident as I would have liked. I lived in fear—of failure, of not being enough, of never being "successful." I was worried about what other people thought of me because I was so judgmental and critical of others. I was always complaining and rarely thankful for the good in my life. I was not taking care of my body and often turned to alcohol to numb myself. I certainly wasn't embracing the idea of self-care or taking time for myself without experiencing a heavy dose of guilt. I neglected to take care of myself and kept myself busy in order to keep me from recognizing what was lacking in my life and how unhappy I was.

Guilt, fear, negativity, poor choices, physical and emotional distress, unhappiness…this was no way to live! I set about slowly becoming more aware of when these negative scenarios surfaced and tried my best to switch the track. It was not easy to change a lifetime of bad habits and crappy thinking, but I made strides. Trying to make changes in life is difficult because our bodies are designed to resist change to protect us. We are comfortable doing the same things over and over, whether it is good for us or not. It's called the comfort zone for a reason.

Until we are aware of something, we cannot change it. We are doing the best we can with what we know, and often we are out of balance. However, often we have no awareness of something that everyone else sees that is negatively affecting our lives. Until we become aware of it, we cannot choose to make a change.

All of this means that awareness becomes the primary challenge. It's about being consciously in the moment and having the courage to honestly ask ourselves clarifying questions such as: Why am I doing this? What do I really want? Why do I complain so much? Why is this person upset with me? What can I do to improve?

I pressed myself to remain aware of the things that needed changing and asking myself when I was triggered, "What is really upsetting you?" I continually examined my reactions to things and started to change those reactions to a more positive and productive way of thinking. I began to share my successes with other women who I then helped to create immense changes in their own lives. They appreciated my authenticity and vulnerability around my failures and the lessons that I was now sharing. It felt amazing to be helping others. I *thought* I was doing great! Unfortunately, my life still wasn't quite balanced, so I regressed to old patterns on several levels without even realizing it.

I was going about my life working seven days a week in a busy and demanding career as a real estate agent, attending events, going to meetings and lunches, nurturing a romantic relationship, and running a household and all the details that come with that job. It was easy to say I was stressed. Then, usher in a four-day hospital stay due to a still-unknown illness. I now consider it divine intervention because they found a mass on my kidney while I was there, which was not what originally sent me to the hospital. I was forced to take some time off, take it easy, and take care of myself—something I had forgotten to do. I went back a few months later to have the mass removed, requiring me to once again slow down and rest. The mass turned out to be a low-grade cancer that thankfully was fully removed without the need for further treatment. I was convinced that the catalyst for this illness was all of the stress of living an unbalanced life where work overpowered everything, causing me to neglect the concepts of self-respect that I knew were so vitally important.

During my weeks of recovery, I began to re-examine where I was in my life and realized that I had become the overworked, underappreciated, bitter woman that my mom once was. I had been teaching this self-respect stuff to other women but hadn't even bothered to really embrace and take my own advice. It had gone in one ear and out the other!

I used my medical leave to explore how I really felt about my real estate career and what was lacking in my life, and I realized how much I longed for a healthier life balance. I had followed my mother's lead into real estate, but I had never been convinced that it was the perfect career for me. After a few years with some great success and a lot of stress, I knew I was good at my job but that something was missing. I questioned if this was my true calling, and deep down I knew that it never was. I had been through some harrowing deals with horrendous clients just prior to my illness and had begun to view my career as a soul-sucking, thankless job. Why the hell would I want to stay in a job like that? The familiar comfort zone of working in real estate kept me there for longer than I should have been. I was fearful of trying to find what else I could do to make that kind of money, even though the money that came in was inconsistent. There had been several months at a time where I made no income at all, forcing me to drain my savings account and go deep into debt in order to survive.

This health calamity became a gigantic wake-up call. It was a re-examination of my life, my soul's purpose, my pursuit of happiness, my life balance, and where my deep self-respect had gotten lost. My bank account was up and down, my moods were up and down, my health was up and down, and the scales had been tipped to the side of overworked rather than being balanced with really taking care of myself and doing what I needed to do in order to be happy.

I decided to come up with a blueprint for getting back on track by creating boundless self-respect. I began to write out all of the tools that I had learned and was teaching to other women. Many of these things were so simple, but I hadn't been fully embracing any of them. I discovered that some of the simple acts of journaling, meditating, boosting my positive self-talk, embracing real self-care and body wellness, and setting and sticking to boundaries were the best ways to honor myself and change my fear and insecurities into confidence and power. As I started re-implementing these tools into my life, I began to feel really good again.

The following is a small sampling of the insights I had while I was developing this blueprint.

I didn't want to settle for less than I deserved, so I had to be clear on what it was that I really wanted. I took some time to consider what mattered most to me by connecting with myself and what was in my heart. The only way to get the life I wanted was to know WHAT I wanted! Once I had more clarity about who I really was, I could better focus on the activities and people that would support me. I visualized exactly what I wanted and made a wild and crazy wish list for my life. I allowed myself to dream and imagine the life I wanted as if all the yucky things had gone away and nothing could stop me. I didn't have any idea how to get there, but that didn't matter. I just needed to know where I was going.

I also reviewed my core values. Of course, respect was and always will be my number one core value, but there were a couple of others at the top of the list as well: authenticity and wellness. These values have toggled around a little bit over the years depending on what is happening in my life. For example, you can imagine with my health crisis that the core value of wellness rose to the upper part of the list. Being clear on my core values is how I could be guided by what I believe in, not by what others think I should do. I needed to embrace those core values every day.

My self-respect needed to be fed, constantly. I found this out when I went on auto-pilot and forgot all the things that I was teaching to others! It's difficult to maintain self-respect based on just a few successes, so I needed to remind myself to stay present and continue to review my blueprint on a regular basis.

Life is not always easy. Experts tell us to think positive and ignore negative thoughts, which is something that is always easier said than done. I was becoming more aware of when I would dip into negativity as a response to my experiences, and I began to actively exchange negative thoughts for positive ones. I found that positive affirmations were a great way to turn my brain around and shift my subconscious mind. I wrote out some specific affirmations about where I wanted to be and who I wanted to be, acting as if I already had achieved them. I repeated them daily and even wrote some of them on my bathroom mirror to remind myself to believe! When I noticed the negative words I was saying about myself, I tried to stop and find an opposite word so that the negative got spun into something positive. I pushed myself to be aware of when I was saying things like "Dang, I look like crap. What kind of animal was sleeping in my hair last night?" Or, when I would make a small mistake or do something stupid, I would say things like, "I'm such an idiot!" I knew that saying those negative things about myself was really having an effect on me. The only way that I could walk out my door every day and be respectful of others was by truly respecting and loving myself, so I had to start speaking to myself with love.

When we learn to truly love ourselves, we can then focus on our health and wellness. One of the exercises in the blueprint included a bit of a body scan. I took some time to consider how I could better respect my skin, hair, nails, teeth, ears, muscles, eyes, gut, heart, and mind. I thought about what I was putting onto my skin and hair. Many personal products and home cleaning products contain chemicals that can be harmful, so I set about removing and replacing a lot of these toxic products. For example, commercial air fresheners and scented candles emit harmful chemicals into the air that we breathe, so I replaced those with all-natural essential oils in a diffuser.

I also thought about what my eyes were seeing. I stayed away from violent and evil movies as well as the news. I listened to more soothing music rather than music that had offensive lyrics. My eyes and ears did not need to absorb this negativity if I wanted to truly embrace self-respect.

I knew that in order to fully respect my body, I would have to examine my nutrition. I began eating foods and drinking beverages that were nourishing rather than harmful. I decided to use organic foods instead of ones that had pesticides, insecticides, and preservatives. Don't get me wrong, though—I believe in all things in moderation, so I'm not opposed to a chocolate sundae or a good cheeseburger when the craving strikes!

Many people turn to alcohol to numb the disappointments and struggles in their lives, as I have done many, many times in the past. I evaluated my alcohol intake and whether I was using it as a crutch or enjoying it in moderation. When we look to alcohol or drugs to numb the feelings we don't like—such as anger, fear, and disappointment—we also numb the good feelings that we do want, like happiness, joy, and love. These numbing agents cannot and will not decipher between the good and bad feelings; if you numb one, you numb them all.

We all know that regular exercise is great for our body and heart health. Finding the right kind of exercise that fits each of us is the key to staying with a regular exercise program, preventing us from getting overwhelmed and quitting altogether. I wrote down exercises that I liked to do and that I thought were fun; they are the ones that I could implement and get full enjoyment out of while also respecting my body. There were also some basic body concepts that I knew would be easy to implement, things like getting enough sleep to fully recharge my battery and start each day refreshed and drinking enough water throughout the day to remain hydrated and cleanse my body.

I recognized that I had not been embracing consistent self-care. I know that self-care can look different to each person, so I made a list of all the potential self-care techniques that I might like to employ. This included things like taking time to meditate—one of the best things we can do, in my opinion— and spending time in nature. Other tasks topping the list were taking time to do some reading for pleasure, journaling, watching a good movie, and taking a nap. I had forgotten to take time for myself without feeling guilty for it, and when I got sick my body sang the chorus of my new theme song loud and clear: "Slow down!"

Taking this self-respect theme to heart meant I would need to set some better boundaries. I had always been a pleaser and a yes-woman. I hated to say no to things and was constantly giving in to my "FOMO," or fear of missing out. I had to learn how to say a very strong "No!" to things that just weren't going to serve me. I had to learn to be okay with disappointing people. I had to be assertive and know that I was doing it to honor myself, and not just doing things to please others.

Speaking of others, I began to evaluate the people that I had surrounded myself with. I wanted to purge the negative influences and embrace those who respected and accepted me for who I was. Negative people were starting to wear off on me, and I was attracting people with a similar state of mind. As I began changing to a more positive frame, I knew that I needed to seek out people who would treat me the way I wanted to be treated, and I could then reciprocate that positivity and respect. And yes, once I knew that I wanted more positive people around me, those people somehow found me and became part of my life!

Another thing I knew I had to let go of was the past, which can be hard. We've all made mistakes, but I had to recognize how to learn the lesson and leave the mistakes behind. I was able to identify where I needed to take responsibility for my mistakes and not blame others so that I could do things differently next time. I thought about the people who had "done me wrong," and I recognized that I needed to forgive them and stop dwelling on it! Forgiveness can be very hard to do, but carrying around hurt feelings and anger makes it even more difficult to have self-love. The pain that others may have caused me was taking up space in my heart and mind, which I would much rather fill with uplifting experiences and people.

Being my true, authentic self was necessary for incorporating more self-respect into my life. I had to stop being what everyone else was expecting me to be and just be ME. This was a challenge, especially around my family. There were always expectations of me and I always wanted to please them, but I knew that ultimately this was not serving me. Why would I want to be anyone else when I *get* to be me every day? I had to stop comparing myself to others, especially on social media where everyone is bragging about everything. I had to remind myself that I really had no idea what was going on behind the scenes in their lives and that no one is perfect. I had to focus on who I truly was and what I had and forget about what other people were doing. I had to stop judging them and stop complaining about my life because complaining just rewires our brains for negativity. In the process, I started to become aware of when I was complaining just to complain. Did I want someone to help me? Or did I just want to vent? We all need to vent sometimes, and that is perfectly normal. However, I noticed there were things in my life that I was constantly complaining about, over and over. Rather than continuing to complain, I had to think about what steps I might be able to take to change what was happening and then STOP complaining!

I kept reminding myself to be confident. Oh sure, just be confident! I put on training wheels for this one by reflecting on the things that I was already confident about and that I knew I was good at. When others would compliment me, I would accept the compliment and take note of when I felt proud. The more I acknowledged my skills and gifts, the more confident I felt. I wanted to love me for me, so I set about writing down all the things that I loved about myself. I already knew all the bad things, the mistakes, and the regrets, but I let them all go and took some time to recognize all the great things about me! And then I gave thanks for my unique gifts that make me who I am.

I had to learn to let go of worry. My mother taught me how to worry—she was, and still is, really good at it. Worry is a very unsettling feeling that tends to feed itself and become a vicious cycle, creating even more things to worry about. I had to be aware of when I was worrying about things that I had no control over. I began to envision my worries becoming little prayers that I could release to the universe. When I couldn't control things with worry, it seemed that praying was about the only thing I could actually DO about it. This made me feel so much better and allowed me to let go of the worry when it would surface.

My mom also taught me how to be strong and put on a happy face, no matter what. As I worked through my journey, I recognized that this tactic was not allowing me to be authentic or vulnerable. I rarely allowed myself to cry when I was upset—I saw it as a sign of weakness—and I certainly wouldn't cry in front of anyone else, probably because I had never seen my mom or dad cry. It was difficult for me to ask for help because I could "do it myself," in the same way that my mom had always been tough and self-sufficient. Allowing others to see us in distress or accepting help during those times would show vulnerability, and I was worried that being vulnerable would make me look stupid and weak. But it turns out that allowing others to see our vulnerability is when true connection takes place. When we hear or see someone else being vulnerable, we start to realize that we are not alone and recognize things that we may not have ever shared with anyone for fear of being judged.

The final part of my blueprint was that I had to take all that I had learned about myself and wrap it up with a gigantic bow of gratitude. I knew that I had to accept all of what was in my life, both the good and the bad, and douse it with huge doses of appreciation and gratitude. Even the bad things in my life had provided me with the opportunity to become a different and better person. Gratitude tends to lead to more generosity and giving, which ultimately creates abundance. The inverse of this is also true—when I was able to offer authentic generosity and more giving, a deep sense of gratitude followed. That is what I call the Gratitude Vortex! I was finally infinitely grateful for what I had and who I was.

A month after my health crisis, I made the difficult decision to leave the real estate industry. I worried about letting my mother down, but thankfully she told me that I could never disappoint her and that she was proud of everything I had done in my life. What a relief that was for my "pleaser" self! It was time to embrace what I felt was my true calling: helping others to overcome fear and insecurities and to find a more inspired life in the same way that I had.

It was hard to trust that leaving real estate was the right decision. It felt crazy to walk away from a good career with semi-steady money, and I was worried about how I would pay the mortgage and my bills. This is where faith came in. I started to remind myself that everything always works out for me; I wasn't sure how, but I knew that it would. After proclaiming out loud that I was "planning" to leave real estate and aligning more with what was tugging at my heart, divine intervention took over and I was amazed at the opportunities and blessings that showed up out of nowhere.

I was chatting with the manager at the radio station where I had been doing a small amount of radio for sixteen years, and he said that they were planning to make some changes in the next couple of months and that they could use my help. This was a perfect way to have at least some kind of steady income to help sustain me while I found my true passion. I was also able to negotiate with my real estate broker to allow me to be a referral agent and collect referral fees for the clients I passed on to other agents within the firm. I was asked to write this chapter out of the blue when I reconnected with a dear friend after almost a year. I was invited to be a speaker at an upcoming women's event and was asked to do an interview about my newly founded entity, The Life Balance Academy. I began to get downloads from my spiritual connection, allowing me to formulate The Life Balance Blueprint program even better than before. And I picked up two new coaching clients almost immediately after making my decision to leave real estate.

I would never have been open to these opportunities if I had remained in a stagnant and unfulfilling career, and they likely would have passed me by. It was all truly divine timing. I knew that making this career change would not be easy, but I was willing and happy to accept the exciting ride to a more fulfilling life. I now know that embracing a balanced life full of deep self-respect, honoring my gut feelings, and having faith is what will boost me into the life I was meant to live.

I encourage you to embrace a deep sense of self-respect by employing some of the tactics I have shared here. I know that even small shifts can make a big difference in how we see ourselves and how we can begin to bring to us the life we have always envisioned. All of this may seem like pie-in-the-sky thinking and difficult to embrace every day, and I hear that loud and clear! But no matter what, always remember that you are beautiful, smart, and powerful, despite the crazy situations you may find yourself in. And remember that I believe in you.

About Sue Bonzell

Sue Bonzell is a radio personality, professional speaker, author of *The Respect Experiment*, and founder of The Life Balance Academy. She has worked for many years in media, marketing, and real estate, but her true passion is making profound personal connections and helping people discover greater happiness and harmony in their lives.

Having experienced struggles that left her life in a bit of a mess, Sue realized it was time for a drastic change. She embarked on an eye-opening journey of personal growth and, after many years of self-discovery, has found the secret to true happiness, contentment, and abundance: living a life built on the foundation of respect.

An engaging and charismatic speaker, Sue enthusiastically brings across this very important concept to her audiences. She has a natural ability to inspire, encourage, and motivate by sharing successful tactics for overcoming hurdles and creating a more fulfilling life and healthier relationships. Her insights are spot on, offering straightforward techniques that are easy to manage yet have a great impact on the lives of her readers and audiences everywhere.

Sue offers the comprehensive Life Balance Mastery Program, tailored to her clients' needs, which helps them complete a blueprint of self-discovery to embrace a life filled with deep self-respect.

www.TheLifeBalanceAcademy.org
Phone: 707-481-9102
Email: TheLifeBalanceAcademy@gmail.com

7

My Blessings, My Journey

by Juanita Figueroa

My Blessings, My Journey

As I reflect upon my journey, I can see the stepping stones that I initially saw as obstacles but can now be viewed as blessings. Each experience served a purpose in my journey to becoming who I am today.

As a Latina born and raised in the Bay Area to teenage parents, I was labeled as just another statistic, one that society would one day consider a liability. My parents did their best to create a loving home, but their foundations crumbled when their childhood pain and learned behaviours began to surface. My father repeated the behaviours he had learned from his father and became a womanizer and an alcoholic who beat the women he claimed to love. My mother desperately wanted us to have a father figure in our life, having never had one herself, and in an attempt to provide this for us she sacrificed her mind, body, and spirit. I was ten years old when my parents finally divorced, and I remember being so excited that my prayers had finally been answered. My mother took us across the states to live in Ohio so that she would be safe from my abusive father, but that only lasted a year. When we moved back to California my mother began to explore the dating world, which was a challenge not only for her but for us as well. I believe her lack of experience and the trauma from her relationship with my father didn't really give her much to stand on. She made some choices that eventually caused her to neglect her children, and being the oldest I had to carry the load. I shared my situation with a teacher at school, and next thing I knew we were being removed from her care. I was placed in a group home, then with a great aunt, and finally with my father. My siblings, on the other hand, were placed back in her care.

As a child I observed my parents' journey mostly through a

lens of anger, hate, judgment, resentment, and disappointment. I made a decision to never be like them, much less marry someone like my father. I recall declaring to my mother that I would never be a teen mom like her. I made a vow to myself that I would never allow anyone to hurt me the way it seemed my mother had allowed my father to hurt her. But being in fear and only focusing on the problem would soon create the very thing I had feared and judged the most.

I was physically young and yet mentally it seemed my life had matured me beyond my years. I had experienced so much in such a short time, so it was no surprise when I met my future husband at the tender age of fifteen. He was older than me by almost three years, had a car, was in college, and had a job, and he soon would teach me what real love felt like. He was shy and mysterious, yet his love for me would radiate. I felt safe and protected, and he showed me a world I had never seen before—a world that was free, fun, and most of all, full of love. I embraced this new life even though it was different, allowing the steel mental wall I had created to protect myself to begin to melt away. I made it clear from the very beginning that I would have zero tolerance of any disrespect, much less any kind of abuse. I was firm, to the point that I could see the fear of losing me in his eyes, yet at the same time he was confident that he could provide me with the life I always longed for and deserved. His confidence gave me a sense of security. Our connection was like no other—an unbreakable forever love. I was happy and in love, and life was great.

I was so completely absorbed in the feelings of security and warmth that I soon found myself making some impulsive decisions that would change my life forever. Just three days after my sixteenth birthday, I was shocked and at a loss for words when I got the news. Did I really recreate my greatest fear? Was I to live the life of my mother? How could I have been so vulnerable? So many emotions ran through me; I could not believe that I was pregnant! Everything was going so well and now, just when I had really started living and enjoying my life for the very first time, I would become a mother. The disappointment of following my mother's footsteps and continuing the cycle was the hardest part of accepting my future. Having my baby was my ONLY choice, and I now had to accept the consequences of my choices. My next chapter had arrived, whether I was ready or not!

My boyfriend was super excited, and he embraced this new journey with open arms. He later told me that he knew from first sight that I would one day be his wife and the mother of his children. I was not at all worried about how we would raise our child or if he would stick around; I trusted that all would work out the way it was meant to be, even if that meant me doing it alone.

The next step was to tell our parents and plan our future. My father, whom I had been living with for a year now, was my first stop in revealing the big news. I waited for a day that he was not drunk—a challenge, since those days were few and far between. Even though my boyfriend offered to go with me, I opted to keep him safe since my father was known to be extremely violent. His reaction was to immediately kick me out at 2:00 a.m., two weeks away from finishing my freshmen high school year. I was devastated and extremely angry at him since this was exactly what he had done to my mother; I guess being on the other side didn't feel so good after all. The day I left, I wrote him a note telling him that he was a coward for turning his back on me for something that he too had done. After he kicked me out, he didn't come to see me or even call to check on me for quite a while. Even when we started talking again, our relationship seemed to always have a distance since it seemed that he only came around to cause pain and hurt.

Then, it was my boyfriend's turn to tell his parents, and their reactions were interesting. His mom was angry, and his dad was worried about how this would all play out.

The last step was for me to tell my mother. I was not looking forward to this conversation since all I could envision her saying to me was "I TOLD YOU SO!" The truth was I was extremely embarrassed and simply didn't want to face her. In the end she didn't react much to the news since we didn't really have a relationship after I had been removed from her care.

This pregnancy was becoming a blessing in disguise as it took me away from my problematic family. I moved in with my boyfriend and his family in their one-bedroom apartment and ended up sleeping on the living room floor for most of my pregnancy. His father supported us with so much love, but his mom didn't care for me one bit and felt the need to make my life impossible. It was emotionally draining and caused many problems within my boyfriend's and my relationship, and we even separated a few times. I eventually realized she had another plan for her son, and I wasn't part of it. I understand that as a mother you only want the best for your child, but even YOU don't know what that is as everyone is on their own individual journey. I wondered if just seeing her son happy was ever going to be enough.

This new chapter brought up a lot of emotions and challenges. As a Mexican-American teen mother, I was once again labeled as just another statistic. I was looked down on from the outside world and judged everywhere I went. I noticed all the comments, felt all the stares, and experienced all the different treatment. This was going to be a long journey, and a very challenging one at that. My steel mental wall was beginning to show itself again as I felt the need to protect myself. I not only had to prove myself to both our moms but also to the entire world, because everyone viewed me as a liability. They all wanted to see me fail, but I was determined to do my very best to prove them all wrong.

I continued going to a school for pregnant teens while living with my boyfriend and his family, and I took all the classes that would teach me how to be the best mommy I could be. I read a lot of books, went to all my doctor visits, and took extra courses at the hospital to make sure I was as prepared as possible. My relationship with my mother began to bloom, since we now had more in common than ever before. As for my father, our relationship was on eggshells; we saw each other on a few occasions, but I was still hurt by the hypocrisy of him punishing me for something he too had done.

My boyfriend was on a mission to provide for us and worked two to three jobs just to make ends meet for our growing family. I spent a lot of time sitting in the car parking lot of the restaurant where he worked as a busboy. Every time he would come check on me, which was quite often, he would bring me some food. He loved to spoil me, and it was beginning to show. My body was changing rapidly—when I first found out I was pregnant I only weighed 130 pounds, and by the time I gave birth I was 210 pounds! This change in my body was more than I could handle, but there was not much I could do.

His father showed us continued love and support by moving us all into a house where my boyfriend and I would have our own room. I spent most of my later pregnancy months in my room sleeping because I was lonely and emotional. I spent a lot of time thinking of how I was going to change the story, and how I could remove the label society had placed upon me.

I made an adult decision that gave me an adult consequence, and now I had to rise to the occasion.

My boyfriend and I lived as though we were husband and wife. He provided and I took care of the room duties as well as doing all I could to make sure our baby would be born healthy and happy. I spent a lot of time reading books to my baby through my belly because I felt it would help make him smart. I wanted more than anything for my son to never feel the consequences of my actions and my choices.

I was in labor for three consecutive days before my baby boy finally blessed us with his presence. My son was the first grandson on both sides of our families and was loved by so many. Everyone came to meet the new addition, embracing him with so much love. For a moment, life seemed so incredibly accepting and amazing. Just before leaving the hospital, though, I was quickly reminded of the label society had placed upon me. An on-duty doctor came in to release me, and before leaving my room he confidently said "see you next year." I was taken aback, hurt, and extremely angry. He automatically assumed I would be back to have another child, just like so many other teens! This was a cycle I didn't want to follow and a label I was determined not to carry for the rest of my life—although it sure seemed to follow me wherever I would go. Interestingly enough, as angry as I was at him for that comment, it gave me more willpower to prove them all wrong, and I decided to see it as a reminder to keep my eye on the fact that I would change the story. So thank you, Doctor, for helping me stay on track in achieving my goal!

My father was also expecting a child with his new girlfriend while I was pregnant, and their daughter happened to be born just three days later. She grew up with my son just as I had grown up with my cousin; it felt like my childhood all over again.

They created an incredible bond and shared many memories together. It's funny how much life had repeated itself, and the amazing thing was that I was aware of it. Awareness is key!

Becoming a mommy to a newborn was a challenge all of its own, one that I couldn't began to understand until I was in it. I gave it my all, but having a baby that relied on me 24/7 left very little room for my relationship, which caused a lot of friction. My boyfriend, who was now working three jobs, became extremely jealous of the baby and felt left out. The baby spent most of his time sleeping and breastfeeding, which also took up most of my time. I was exhausted as my body was still trying to heal and everyone seemed to need something from me. A big gap was starting to form in our relationship. He was used to getting all my attention but now he had to not only share it, he had to give it up due to working three jobs. It caused us to have more conflict in our relationship, and I started to become overprotective.

Part of the reason that I had become so overprotective was that I believed that if I could put fear into my boyfriend, it would guarantee that he would never try to strike me. Even though he never showed signs of being abusive and did not come from that kind of background, I did and that was enough for me to believe it was possible. I took it to the extreme in hopes that I would never be hurt or overpowered by a man the way my mother had. I soon realized that I did not respect the role of a father whatsoever because I didn't experience one in my own childhood, so how would I begin to understand the value? Plus, the reality was that I was prepared to walk this journey alone and do it all by myself, so much so that I expected to. I had watched my mother do it, so I assumed that it was the way it would eventually be for me as well. I made sure to always keep my independence by not losing who

I was. I continued my education and did my best to create value in myself by investing in my life experiences. I tried new things and used my creativity to new levels. I began creating handmade items for upcoming parties and building strong and loving relationships with family and friends.

However, no matter how much I pushed my boyfriend away, he persisted, and I began to see how much he valued me and our little family. He made adjustments so that he could keep us together. He had patience, and most of all he had an abundance of love for ME, to the point that it became overwhelming. He smothered me with it, so much so that I felt I couldn't breathe. I now realize that it was the only way he could crack that hard shell, that steel wall I had created. In the beginning, I reminded him often that I didn't mind walking this journey with my son alone, and his response was always the same: "I know!" It started as a test to see his reaction, and to confirm if his love was truly unconditional. Then it became a declaration that I was not going to be taken advantage of, and that I was not afraid to be alone. They say love conquers all, and so it did. No matter what I did or said, he loved me unconditionally.

During those early days, I reacted to even the smallest of things because I figured that if I barked the loudest, I would become the scariest. I wanted him to fear my reaction as a way to protect myself, but I never stopped to realize that I could actually be hurting him. He never liked confrontation, much less arguing—I did most of that all by myself. He never said much until the dust would settle, and then he would simply say "I am sorry." It confused me because I thought he was supposed to argue back, then get violent, followed by chaos everywhere, but he would only listen. I purposely would push buttons and throw low blows, but still he would not react. I realized that he had been teaching me all along how to respond and how not to react, once again through patience and unconditional love. I began questioning the thoughts behind all my actions, and I became embarrassed and ashamed of how I had reacted. I mean, if you really love someone, then why would you treat them this way? I was becoming the very person I was afraid he would be.

Every new stage in our journey brought up new triggers that I had to learn to work through. In order to overcome the limiting beliefs I had learned in my childhood, I started by validating my feelings and thoughts, then challenging them with the actual truth. I could choose to see things for what they truly were by stopping and asking myself what was really happening, then focusing on the truth of what was really going on by being honest with myself. Little things my boyfriend would do, like being tired all the time and being gone a lot, would trigger my childhood memories of how my father was during my parents' marriage, which had turned out to be a rap sheet of infidelities. However, my boyfriend was not my father. He never showed any signs of hurting me, physically or mentally, so why did I continue to be triggered? I questioned it a lot and wondered if I would ever be able to shake it off.

My boyfriend patiently allowed me to come to the reality that my fear and judgment of my father had manifested in me, and that this was not okay—a sad and embarrassing truth. I had to admit to myself that I was wrong and that I had to change, or I would run the risk of losing the very person I loved. The mean, angry, overprotective, independent young woman I had become would get me nowhere if I truly wanted to succeed in this life. I asked him to forgive me for I didn't know any better, but now that I did I would work hard to do better and be better. I had to learn to trust him in order to completely remove my wall; after all, he had been trustworthy this entire time.

Standing in my truth through my own reality, I realized that the old me no longer suited who I was becoming and the chapter I was entering. I had no more reason to be angry, mean, and overprotective. I was being rebuilt, retaught, and recreated, and although it felt weird, it also felt so empowering. I was gaining a new independence and learning that I had many reasons to be happy, and that I needed to start fully enjoying life. It took a lot of discipline to change my mindset, both mentally and emotionally, as thoughts and feelings continued to arise from the judgments I had had about my mother. They made me feel like I was losing my independence, which would bring up feelings of weakness and inadequacy. It felt like I was being stripped of all my armour, but that was not the truth. The truth was that it felt good to finally enjoy life. I worked through each limited belief, calling it what it was and exposing the truth of it all. The radar in me was still working, so if at any point I felt I could be unsafe I knew what to do. I had nothing to worry about, though, since there were no signs of danger.

I eventually learned a new way of being without the fear, only love and trust. I was maturing and healing from my childhood trauma all while raising my own baby. I took pride in learning how to become a great woman, mother, and eventually wife. I was on my way to giving my son a new and prosperous life, one that would be different from mine. I had many issues compared to my boyfriend as I had lived a different life than him, but my experiences served a purpose, as did his. We were both learning; this life was new for him too. He embraced the challenge and allowed the space for us to mature through our limiting beliefs, and as I grew, so did he.

My boyfriend had his own set of challenges, and at one

point I felt equipped to help him through them. However, this only seemed to cause more friction between us. I learned that we cannot be our partner's shrink or try to fix them, but we can support them as we lead the way through our own healing. We must allow their journey to unfold in their own divine timing. As I gained a new and deeper respect for myself, he began to see his own. Stepping into a new workplace, vulnerable and scared of the unknown, he found an amazing opportunity that changed our lives forever. He discovered a new love for semi-trucking and travelling the world, one that created security and abundance for our family.

I made sure we could get through this challenging and growing chapter before even considering marriage, although in the Latin culture you are considered married once you live together or have a baby. I noticed many teen moms automatically married or were forced to marry the baby's father when they became pregnant, but I was not going to be part of that. I wanted to build a solid foundation with choices, not obligations or expectations. Now that we had a solid relationship, the next obstacle to overcome was one I was not expecting: I found out my husband was not legal in this country. He was brought here by his parents at a young age so he could have a better life. This meant that if we got married, we would have to go through an extensive process to ensure he was legally able to provide for our family. Even with this new obstacle I would only choose to marry him for love, not because he was my baby's father or because of his legal status. He was and is still the love of my life.

When we finally married, our son walked down the aisle as our ring bearer, and we went on to have a honeymoon with our son by our side. Our week away was magical and filled with love and support, the perfect start to a new chapter. We gradually achieved our full independence, getting our first apartment with just the three of us—a huge accomplishment that I longed for. Living on our own was a huge challenge because we had to solely rely on each other, so I began to work outside the home to help ease the load as independence was not cheap. Celebration was soon in order as my husband's legal status had finally changed, and he was now a citizen of the United States.

Life had finally settled into place, so we decided it was time to have a second child. Everything was great—our jobs were good and our home life was incredible. This was our very first planned pregnancy, and my first time doing everything right. I had a job, a husband, and a home, and we were completely independent, everything society tells you must have in place to have a child.

It took a bit of time, but soon enough I was pregnant. I remember feeling different from the very beginning but brushed it off because I thought it was because we were in a different space in our lives. Deep down, though, I knew the different feeling was from the pregnancy itself. I did my best to ignore the feeling, but then I woke up one night out of the blue and had to run to the bathroom. This must have startled my three-year-old son, because he came running after me and hugged me tight. He assured me everything would be okay, and at first I didn't understand why he would say that. Then, when I got up from the toilet I screamed—to my surprise, there was a thick red puddle of blood. My husband came running in and called the doctor. I was assured that everything was okay, and for a while that was true. But many weeks later, when I was about five months along, we found out our baby had died in utero. I could not grasp the fact that we had lost our baby, the one we had planned and done everything right for. I didn't want to accept it. My son knew something was wrong and tried to console me often. I was devastated and cried for months, grieving the loss of my baby while holding the only outfit I had bought hoping it would be a girl. I was angry with the world. How could I do everything right and still lose my baby when there were people out there that didn't even want their children? I went to a very judgmental place as I couldn't understand why this would happen to me. I was a mother of two but had only one child here on earth with me.

A year later the opportunity to buy our first home came up, so we went for it. This new chapter was a drastic change involving moving cities, being away from any and all family, and starting fresh. It was a challenge, but with my son starting school soon I wanted a home in an area where he could go to school and grow up with his childhood friends. It would be a forever home that would be filled with lifetime memories. We soon met new people and created our own family in a town where we had none.

Another year later, when my son was six years old, we were surprised to find out we were expecting once again. This pregnancy was full of fears and triggers from the previous traumatic pregnancy. I wanted so much to believe that all would be okay, but my worry and doubt continued to surface. I did my best once again to protect myself and my baby—I even moved into the room on the first level to avoid the stairs as a safety precaution. This pregnancy was very delicate and scary, but thankfully my second son arrived healthy and happy, a blessing that I had longed for. Eventually, I came to the realization that had we had our baby three years prior, we may not have had the opportunity to buy this home due to the extra expenses. This gave me a sense of relief and an increased strength in trusting that life is always happening for us, not against us.

All the sacrifices and all the growing we have done along the way has taught us that everyone has a choice no matter what their past, and that moving forward is always an option. Taking this path may not be easy but it is definitely worth it.

Today, I am still married to the love of my life and my family has grown, becoming The Figueroa Bunch. Another three years after having my second son, I was surprised to be pregnant again with a baby girl. She is currently fifteen and anxiously awaiting her quinceñera. My boys are now twenty-four and eighteen and are enjoying creating their own life experiences. The newest additions were through adoption—a set of brothers who are currently twenty-seven and nineteen. Every challenge I have faced through this amazing journey has contained an incredible amount of growth, as my children are my greatest teachers.

For me, life is all about the journey, not the destination. I am grateful for all of my life experiences, and most of all for my strength in overcoming them. Life is not about perfection but about living to the fullest. Take control of your journey and rise!

About Juanita Figueroa

Juanita Cruz-Figueroa is a Mexican-American Latina born and raised in San Jose, California. Born to teen parents, she is the oldest of four siblings and became a second-generation teen mother at the age of sixteen. She is currently married to her husband of twenty-three years and is the mother of five children—four boys and one daughter—two of which were adopted.

Outside of her family life, Juanita is a Spiritual and Intuitive Guidance Coach. Her accomplishments include being a Certified Life Coach, a Master Angelic Card reader, a Certified Reiki Healer and an Ordained Minister. She studied psychology in college and carries a passion for guiding people and helping them reconnect to their love of life.

www.guidancebyjuanita.com
Email: balancinglifesflow@gmail.com
Facebook: Guidance by Juanita
Instagram: @guidancebyjuanita

8

Shattering the Internal Glass Ceiling

by Wanda King

Shattering the Internal Glass Ceiling

As a young woman in the '80s, I recall the struggle I faced in securing advancement in corporate America—an experience shared by many, many women at the time. Women were regarded as too weak or too soft to be in leadership positions and certainly were not valued contributors outside of the home. We were not given the same opportunities for career advancement, education, or even simply having a voice in this world. Society coined this phenomenon as hitting the "glass ceiling." According to Dictionary.com, the term refers to an "unacknowledged and ultimately illegal barrier to advancement, especially for women and people of color." In many professions today, women are still unable to break through the glass ceiling and achieve senior management positions. Why in the twenty-first century are we still experiencing this behavior from the world?

Although the concept of the "glass ceiling" may have developed in the '80s, I believe women have battled against this same barrier throughout our entire existence.

Throughout history, women have experienced various forms of oppression from parents, siblings, clergy members, teachers, friends, classmates, spouses, and other type of relationships that unintentionally or intentionally create negative impressions in their lives and offer little to no personal growth. For example, think about if you were ever told any of the following: "You can't do that, that's a man's job." "Women don't go to college, men do so they can take care of their families." "Women stay home and take care of the children." "Sit down, be quiet, be a lady." "You need to lose weight so you can attract a man." The list goes on and on.

Eventually, these experiences become our paradigms, our

reality of what we believe about ourselves and how we develop into who we are and how we are perceived by others. We may not recall exactly what happened, but our mind does a great job of reminding us how those experiences impacted us when we think about attempting something we have never done, repeating these negative statements over and over. I call it the "sabotaging voice," and it fills our thoughts with all the reasons why we will never succeed. "You're not good enough." "Don't do it, you will fail." "Give up, you will never get that promotion." "You are too fat, just stay home." If we are not speaking valued messages to ourselves, then how can we expect to speak our value outwardly to the world? We have ultimately created our own internal "glass ceiling."

This was my life for many years—a life of simply surviving, a life where I thought I did not deserve to be happy, or to have a healthy and loving relationship, or career success, or abundance. I later discovered the one common denominator that kept my existence in survival mode instead of a thriving mode: ME!

In fact, looking back on my life, I can now see that I was responsible for the outcomes of all my experiences. Yes, I said it! Trust me, I have had some experiences in which I felt like a victim. I certainly didn't ask to have abusive relationships, or car accidents, or near-death experiences, or any other event that impacted my life negatively.

I am here to say that we do have choices in how we move through all our experiences. Once you decide that you are no longer going to accept the barriers the internal glass ceiling places before you—barriers you have allowed to restrict you throughout the years—it is only then that you will have made the decision to take back control of your life and are able to create a life you want for yourself.

We must decide that we will no longer allow that sabotaging voice to stay in the driver's seat of our life—the voice that devalues us, demotivates us, and destroys any hope of us having the kind of life we have only dreamed of having. If we do not stand up and make conscious choices about what we want, we will always be a VICTIM and never the VICTOR!

Before I jump into how I shifted from merely surviving to shattering my internal "glass ceiling" and living a thriving life where I create my own experiences, I should probably share my story of how I overcame a life of paralyzing fear and became a Mindset Transformation Coach, helping others to rediscover their authentic self and foster unlimited possibilities that result in complete confidence, self-love, self-acceptance, authentic joy, abundance, and all of the amazing things we are meant to have.

I grew up in a small town on the Florida coast as the eldest of three children and the only girl. My childhood years are a bit of a blur up until I left home at the age of eighteen. Perhaps I chose to block out a majority of that time; a time that was anything but safe and nurturing.

From an outsider's perspective, we looked like a normal, middle-class family. Both of my parents worked full-time jobs, we lived in a small home on the outskirts of town, my mother kept the house clean and made the meals for the family, and my brothers and I went to school. We were well-behaved in public and appeared to be a happy family, but what took place inside our house was a very different story.

Ever since I can recall, my father would explode in rages of anger, screaming, and shouting dehumanizing names at my brothers or myself; whoever was in his line of fire would be his target. It was not uncommon to be yanked up and thrown across the room, which would be followed with physical beatings and more screaming of devaluing words. These episodes were unpredictable as we never knew what would trigger them, so we just did our best to avoid him as much as possible. My brothers and I never spoke of the abuse we went through as children; we didn't dare let anyone know for fear of retribution.

Every day when we would come home from school, I would start watching the clock. Just before 4:00 p.m. (the time my father would get home from work), I would gather my brothers and we would hide somewhere outside so we would not be in the house when he walked through the front door. We sometimes made a game out of it; every time we made it outside without him knowing, we felt like we escaped jail and were free, at least for a small window of time.

In addition to my father's abuse, my father and mother argued a lot and had many fights throughout my childhood. Sometimes huge fights would break out at the dinner table and my mother would throw the plates down the hall, smashing as they soared past me to hit my father. Often during those seemingly never-ending battles, my father would yell that my mother hated me and never wanted me. I felt like I was the reason that they were fighting. After hearing these statements time after time at such an impressionable age, I developed a sense of fear, abandonment, and loneliness which later becomes my internal glass ceiling.

During this time, I felt alone. I had no friends and no one to rescue me from the life I was given. My mother and I were not close; she spent much of her time being a mother to my brothers and doing her best to protect them from my father's anger. She never comforted me or made me feel safe and protected like my brothers did. In fact, there were times where I was in the crosshairs of her anger and wrath as well. I didn't understand why I was not treated with the same love she had for my two brothers until I was about twelve or thirteen years old. My mother and I were in a heated argument and she began beating me with a belt and stated she wished she never had me— the very words I heard throughout my life from my father. At least when my father said it, I could somewhat rationalize it and think it wasn't true. Now, there was no more denying it. My life was filled with hopelessness, and I was stuck in this horrible existence with no hope of escape.

A few years later, my parents divorced and I ended up living with my mother and brothers. Life there was strained and I never felt like I was part of the family nucleus, so as soon as I turned eighteen I left home to begin a new life.

A girlfriend and I rented a small apartment in a shady neighborhood. I found a job as a cashier where I made $2.10 per hour, and there were many nights where all we had to eat was popcorn. Having a life with scarcity was still better than my life as a child. However, I continued to battle with my inner sabotaging voice that was constantly telling me I wasn't good enough, I would never be truly happy, I didn't deserve to have good things in my life, and so on. I lived with this controlling inner voice from the moment I woke up until I laid my head down to sleep.

There was only one waking moment that I did not experience those devaluing and demotivating chants in my head. Just prior to moving out on my own, I discovered that a local airport offered skydiving lessons. I went to the airport filled with fear and anxiety, and of course that sabotaging, nasty voice was telling me everything that would go wrong. I finally came to the conclusion that it was worth the risk and took my first static line jump at 2,500 feet. This was the only time in my daily life that I did not hear that sabotaging voice telling me what a loser I am. Without that negative chatter, I felt like

I could do anything. My confidence soared, I had clarity of the moment, and my decisions were deliberate; there was no second guessing if I made the right choice. I felt free from the anxiety and stress that constantly haunted me throughout the day. Instead, I felt euphoric joy, just living in the present moment without judgement, without worry, without doubt. It was more than knowing my life depended on being present enough to pull the ripcord—I was truly living and thriving in the moment. Needless to say, I was hooked!

As I progressed in the sport, I went from a few seconds of freefall and a couple of minutes under a parachute floating through the air to sixty seconds or more in freefall and ten minutes or longer floating under my multicolored parachute! Never once during those heavenly rides did I worry about paying the bills, or how I don't fit in, or how I don't matter, or any other self-sabotaging message. For those few moments in time I felt joy, freedom from fear, and complete control of my world. However, as soon as I landed safely back at the airport, the negative chattering would start up again. I jumped as much as I could on my meager budget to have the peace this amazing sport brought to me, never realizing why that negative voice was not able to penetrate this cherished moment in time.

Unfortunately, my life didn't get much better after I left home. I had thought that I would never be treated the way my parents had treated me if I moved away from them, but the men I attracted were abusive—there was more beatings, more controlling, and no voice. At nineteen, I was married to a man who almost took my life. He held me captive and beat me for eight hours, stating I would not live to see daylight. I survived and divorced him after only six months of marriage, still searching for something or someone to tell me that I mattered, and that I wasn't invisible. I wanted to belong, and I wanted to know I was valued and loved, but my efforts to find these things just brought me more of what I didn't want—more abuse, more abandonment, no joy, and no hope. As I moved into my late twenties, I was still no happier, no more successful, and no wiser than when I left home!

In addition to skydiving, I began to explore a new form of parachuting called B.A.S.E. jumping. The acronym refers to jumping from buildings, antennae towers, spans (bridges), and earth (mountains/rocks), and the sport leaves no room for error. Most jumps are from low altitudes, leaving you only one chance to get it right. B.A.S.E jumping is a sport that you either love or move on from. I was attracted to the sport after hearing about my friends' experiences, but my first jump was one of sheer terror. I climbed a 1,150 ft tower at 10:30 p.m. It took about one hour to climb, which meant one hour of hearing that negative chatter, and the payoff was only about five seconds of freefall and a minute or two under canopy. The jump just didn't give me what skydiving provided me, but I wanted to be fair and try a few more times before deciding it wasn't for me.

When I was twenty-nine years old, I went to my doctor for a routine PAP smear. However, the results were not so routine. They showed I was in the beginning stages of cervical cancer, and I was scheduled for a complete hysterectomy for the following month. That day never came.

The following week, on March 22, 1988, I set off to make my third B.A.S.E. jump. My friends and I decided to launch from a modified parasail that would be pulled by a boat. The jumper would wear a packed parachute and hold on to the inflated parasail until they reached the right height. Then, the jumper would release the parasail, open the packed parachute on their back, and glide safely into the water. Sounds easy enough, right?

After two of my friends successfully landed, it was my turn.

Unfortunately, something went terribly wrong. I released the parasail and attempted to open the parachute on my back, but it did not open. I fell approximately two hundred feet and smashed into four feet of water at eighty miles an hour (water, by the way, is not as forgiving as one may think). At the moment I hit, I saw a bright, white light, and then a loud voice inside of me screamed, "NO! OPEN YOUR EYES AND SHUT YOUR MOUTH!!" I followed the instructions instinctively, and I managed to stay conscious. For the entire time it took to get me out of the water and to the hospital, that same voice chanted, "Keep talking, dead people can't talk." That voice is what kept me alive. I knew I was dying—I could feel my Spirit pulling from my body—but every time I heard that voice, I would say whatever came out of my mouth. I didn't have the energy to filter myself, so I am sure some colorful expletives flew out in the mix!

I was airlifted to a high-tech hospital in Orlando that could handle life-threatening injuries such as mine. I had multiple fractures to my vertebra, both kidneys almost imploded on impact, I was bleeding internally, and I was paralyzed from the waist down—I was labeled an incomplete paraplegic and was later informed by my surgeon that I would never walk again. I was taken into surgery, where my life was touch and go, but I pulled through.

Two weeks after surgery, I had a life-changing near-death experience. I was lying in my bed taking blood transfusions when I saw a man standing at my hospital room door and staring at me with the most loving eyes and beautiful smile. He started walking towards me, his eyes still fixed on mine, without speaking to anyone else in the room. Once he was standing next to me I weakly said, "Hi there," and a nearby family member asked me who I was talking to. It was then that I realized that no one else could see this person.

Minutes after this experience, for lack of a better explanation, I was in a place where I was able to run and jump, completely healthy and filled with love and joy. Then, I looked down and saw my lifeless body lying on that hospital bed. I was so confused; I had no memory of what happened to me. I recall asking, "What's wrong with me? Why are they crying? Why am I lying there?" Right after I said that, I was back in my broken body and fighting for my life. After this experience, I knew without a doubt that I would walk again, but it wasn't until sometime later that I recognized the real gift that I was given by this near-death experience—I could once and for all give up on a life of surviving and FEAR and live a thriving life in radiant joy and peace!

About one month after my accident, I remembered to mention my cervical cancer diagnosis to the nurse. Shocked, she ran out of the room to report the news, and then tests confirmed that I had the pre-stages of cervical cancer. However, since I was in a high-tech hospital, they had cutting-edge procedures that could treat the cancer without requiring a complete hysterectomy. About two weeks after informing the nurse of my diagnosis, I underwent a procedure that removed the cancer from the wall of my cervix. I was told that the damage left from the surgery meant that my cervix would not be strong enough to carry a child, but the procedure was less invasive than a hysterectomy and the long-term effects would be much better than having to be on permanent medications.

After three months in the Humana Lucerne Hospital, the time had come to say goodbye. I was discharged in June 1988, and in spite of what I was told by the doctors, I walked out of the hospital. Since then, my life has been a series of amazing events, some great and others great lessons to learn from.

In March 1989, I became pregnant. Between my back

injuries and my weakened cervix, I was considered a high-risk pregnancy and was referred to a perinatal specialist. There were a couple of times I came close to losing my baby, but on November 20, 1989 I delivered an eight-pound fifteen-ounce baby girl—a miracle indeed! My daughter is now twenty-nine years old and married to a wonderful man, and she is a new mommy to a beautiful baby girl who I absolutely adore.

After having my daughter, I went on to work at Kennedy Space Center in Florida and completed a bachelor's degree in computer information science. I was then offered a position with a prominent software company in California, where I worked for several years. However, I was not content with spending my career in high-tech fields; I felt something was missing. I wasn't living my purpose, and while I wasn't sure exactly what that was, I knew it had something to do with helping others to cultivate a self-awareness about how much they matter and are valued. A few years later I went on to receive a master's degree in organizational management and became the founder of Discover Clear Vision Coaching as a certified Mindset Transformation Coach. I also became a public speaker, sharing my story and strategies through my program series called "From Fear to Fierce: The Power of Inspired Thinking."

Looking back, the accident was the best thing that has ever happened to me. Without the accident, I would have followed through with the planned hysterectomy and I never would have had my beautiful daughter. I also would have never discovered the secret that all human beings must know: to live a thriving life instead of merely surviving.

The key to defeating the inner saboteur and smashing through the internal glass ceiling is quite simple to grasp but difficult to achieve. Through my experiences, I learned three valuable lessons.

Lesson #1: Our Spirit only lives in the present tense, never in the past or future. When I had my out-of-body experience, I had no memory of my accident. That's because I was in Spirit, not in body or mind. Later, it came to me that our Spirit, which lives within us, only lives in PRESENT TENSE! It wasn't until I returned into my body that my mind engaged and I remembered what happened to me.

Lesson #2: Our fear and our inner saboteur only live in the past and future tenses, never the present. It lives in a time that no longer exists. When I was skydiving, I was living in the moment. This is why my sabotaging voice would disappear during these moments; fear could not penetrate the NOW.

Lesson #3: You MATTER. All life matters to the great creator, God, but you also matter to everyone who is close to you. It is only our past that tells us we do not matter. Get out of the past and BE.

Most people spend too much time stressing, worrying, judging themselves and others, and living from a fear-based mindset. This behavior only comes from old stories or paradigms that others created for us, or that we created for ourselves. Our fear latches onto these and keeps us from having experiences of living in the moment—from the present tense.

How do we take control and smash our internal glass ceiling? Here are four steps you can begin immediately to live a thriving life in the present:

1. **Cultivate self-awareness** and change the negative thoughts to positive self-acknowledgements, such as "I am Love," "I am intelligent," "I am the creator of my masterpiece," "I am a Spiritual Being having a human experience," and "I am a product of my Divine Creator." Additionally, listen to your body. If you feel bad, you are not living in the present. If you feel good, do more to

feel good—you are in the sweet spot of thriving in the moment.

2. **Be in gratitude** and recognize what you are thankful for in the moment. Create a habit of doing this throughout the day, as being in gratitude anchors you to the present.

3. Strengthen your **connection to God** through prayer, meditation, and fellowship with others with positive mindsets such as churches, spiritual organizations, or nature; anything that brings that connection of union between you and the Divine Creator.

4. Allow **forgiveness** for yourself and others. My thriving life began when I was able to surrender all the hurt and forgive those who were part of these experiences, including myself.

Fear is nothing more than **F**ocused **E**nergy **A**round **R**esistance , feeding off old stories to keep you frozen in the past. If you want to have a thriving life in all areas, you must move away from the past tense and live in the NOW from a place of **F**ocused **E**nergy **A**round **R**esistance!

As you journey towards living a thriving life, remember that people and things do not define you; you define yourself. What you speak inwardly to yourself is what the world will see about you. Allow yourself to be perfectly incomplete and know you are still working on your masterpiece. Have the courage to take risks—the more you can prove that your inner saboteur is lying to you, the more your confidence will shine through. It's also important to take time for yourself. Read uplifting books, listen to joyful music, and have lunch with a close friend.

The more you stop living in the past and future and start living in the present, the more you realize that you DO matter and have a purpose to share your joy and love with the world.

Then, when fear rears its ugly head, you will have the strength and the power to send fear packing. Make today your beginning to a life of radiant joy.

About Wanda King

Wanda King is a Certified Mindset Transformation Coach who lives her life not as a survivor but instead from a thriving mindset. However, it wasn't always like this. Wanda has had her share of tragedy throughout her life, including abusive relationships, surviving cancer twice, and having near-death experiences. She was at rock bottom with no hope of ever having a life of contentment until she had a divine encounter during a near-death experience that changed her life forever! She discovered how to achieve a life of joy, success, and love by living in the now.

Wanda partners with women and uses proven strategies and transformational workshops to empower them to discover their voice, their value, and their purpose by smashing though their internal glass ceiling—that negative voice from within that devalues, demotivates, and destroys any hope of communicating their value and having the success they want in their life.

If you are ready to own your power and make a difference for yourself and the world, contact Wanda through any of the methods provided below.

www.DiscoverClearVision.com
Email: wanda@discoverclearvision.com
Facebook: Discover Clear Vision

9

Finding My Feminine Fire

by Nina Luchka

Finding My Feminine Fire

What happened to me? Where did I go? No one told me that I'd slowly lose myself and my self-worth if I didn't watch it. No one told me that I would feel like I was unappreciated, but I would still have to keep going and doing the same things over and over. No one told me HOW having a baby, or two, or four, would smother that internal fire—my Feminine Fire. I am one of the strongest people I know, and yet I let myself disappear. How did this happen? How *in the world* did this happen?

Before I had kids, I competed in fitness competitions against the best in the world, winning an All North American show and achieving my professional status with the International Federation of Bodybuilding (IFBB). The determination and perseverance from that experience alone taught me how to build a fitness business and to be a go-getter and a strong person. I created a successful business training clients through online workouts and nutrition recommendations, getting them to achieve their goals and step on stage. I was a powerhouse. I took time for myself daily—doing mediation, eating healthy, exercising, and reading empowering books. Life was amazing!

In December 2008, I found out I was pregnant. There was so much joy and excitement—my husband and I were going to be proud parents! Everyone goes on and on about how things change once you have children, but I wondered if that was really true. I could see that our lives would need to be altered a bit, and that our days would become a juggling act. However, I am the kind of person that is determined to deal with anything that comes my way. I was told there would be days that I wouldn't get to shower and that shopping trips would now be mostly for the kids. Well, those are all little things, and I have always been able to make things work. Always! I was also told that finding a sitter would be easy, so I knew we should be able to get help when we needed it.

My husband and I bought our first house when I was four months pregnant. It was perfect! We had over an acre of land, an in-ground pool, a barn, and lots of room to have a garden. I envisioned a treehouse, goats, horses, and even dirt bikes. We would have the country life and raise country kids, and thinking about this warmed my heart. We started renovations on the house and were about 80% done before our baby arrived. Throughout my pregnancy I was also still training clients and doing tans and makeup for fitness shows. Everything was amazing. I was READY for this baby!

A month and a half before I was due, I took time off of work to focus on the renovations and prepare for my first born. This was happening during the slow season for competitions, which worked out perfectly. Finally, at the end of that month and a half, my precious little baby girl arrived! I was overwhelmed. I was amazed. I was in love. Honestly, words just cannot express the immense LOVE I had for this tiny baby. I had a pretty good experience during delivery, and the hospital staff were incredible. My husband was my ROCK—comforting me, getting ice chips, giving his arm for me to squeeze, and just being attentive to my needs. The whole experience was incredible. In the first few weeks after I arrived home, I would sit with Aspen in my arms and I would just cry tears of joy and beauty on and off for a good hour or two. I was excited and ready to show this little girl the world. I would show her how to be a strong and confident person full of passion and wonder. I would show her how to be independent, curious, and a go-getter. I was so eager to teach her about the universe and the human body and how AMAZING they both are, and to show her that she is here for a purpose. These are all things that

I taught myself over the years after losing my mom to ovarian cancer in 2001—I had started getting anxiety and panic attacks a year after her death, and I had turned to books and nutrition to resolve this problem. Who knew that this was going to be the catalyst for my holistic journey?

Two weeks after the arrival of my little girl, I began to contact clients so I could start getting them ready for shows. I sent out emails to get everyone booked in only to get responses back saying they were covered and didn't need any. Only a few of my close clients said they needed and wanted my services. I was beside myself, wondering what was happening. After a few days of confusion and a little panic, I got an email from one client that said, "Hi Nina, I just wanted to let you know that X has sent out emails telling everyone that you are no longer training people or doing tans and makeup because of the baby, and that SHE has taken over your business."

I felt like I just gotten slammed with a bat and knocked flying down to the ground. I can see it all slow motion—the impact, the hit, me dropping to the floor. There was confusion, panic, and tears. I had a new baby, new house, renovations that needed to be completed, and no business. Almost all of my income was GONE. This was my first hit, and it was such a HUGE hit that I never expected. What started as a time of joy with my newborn became months and months of tears, worry, and the disappearance of a chunk of my self-worth. I tried hard over the next year to build the business back without any luck. Because I wasn't competing anymore I wasn't in the fitness spotlight, and so clients quickly moved on to the next best trainer. My time and energy were now entirely being spent on this precious little baby.

People later asked me why I didn't go after this person for taking my business, and truth be told I was too occupied with the pain, hurt, and sadness to even think about it. Once I was in a place that I could pursue this option, I realized that destroying someone's income didn't sit right with me, no matter what the circumstances. So, I let it go and tried to move on.

Taking care of our child was also more challenging than my husband and I had expected. Contrary to what I had been told, we had an incredibly difficult time finding a sitter and eventually gave up looking for one. There were many sleepless nights and missed meals as I continued pumping, feeding, and caring for my sweet angel with no breaks. There were not as many workouts and not much time for myself, so my whole identity had become being a mom. I was at least able to teach a bootcamp class a couple times a week, which was great for me. I LOVE connecting with women and helping them reach their goals.

I found myself wondering, is this how it's supposed to be? Are things supposed to change this much? How am I going to get back my business, or to the income I had? Life can get tough when you only have one income, and now, three years later, I was having baby number two; a little boy, Cruz. Once again, I was BEYOND excited. And once again, I was incredibly grateful and thankful. My soul was just so happy to have another beautiful soul to teach about this journey we call life.

When I was pregnant with my son, I was offered the opportunity to get back into business and host my own fitness competition. Thank you, Universe! I jumped on board and things were starting to look up. I now had a bit of an income coming in—not much, but something is better than nothing—but the most important thing was that I was regaining some of my feelings of self-worth. Now, I don't want to sound like I don't care about my kids. They are EVERYTHING to me, so much so that I started to lose myself—not entirely, but I felt like at least half of who I was went missing. However, I am a business gal! I need to feel accomplished and challenged in self-employment to feel like myself, and hosting this show was exactly what I needed.

The show ran for about four to five years, and it was great. Amazing, actually. That is, until the show was moved to my business partner's hometown about an hour away from the original location without my consent. I was in a panic because I knew this new location wasn't going to work. It was farther away from a major city, so we wouldn't be able to get the same numbers out and the show would be a loss—one that I couldn't afford. And I was right. That extra little income I was making didn't come that year. Then, the day after the show, my business partner emailed me to tell me she was taking the show and wished me luck with whatever I did next. I was beside myself. I contacted her asking to share the cost of the trophies we had ordered for the show, but there was no response. I was now stuck with paying the bill, which was a few thousand dollars.

I had no show, no income, three kids now, and a hefty bill of trophies to be paid off. Here comes that baseball bat taking me down yet again, and I still hadn't recovered from the last one. For months afterward I couldn't even talk about the show without bawling. I felt worthless. I felt like a loser. I felt defeated by life. How could this happen, twice? I had three beautiful kids and I was trying to be the strongest person they knew, but I was often in tears. I wasn't depressed and I wasn't giving up, my body was just getting rid of the toxic negative emotions that had built up. This is how strong a woman is—she can get hit hard by life and still keep going.

With the business gone I was back to spending all my energy on my kids, and as much as I love being around them I do need mental breaks just to clear my mind. It was tough to have no sitter, no family to help, and a husband who was self-employed and sometimes worked long hours. Even when he was home, I would still stay and help him with the children instead of going out for a little me time because I knew how tough it was to be by yourself with three young, active kids. Plus, they were a lot of fun to be around, and I did love spending time with them.

I needed to figure out this mom thing, though, because baby number four was on the way. Even with all the struggles, the complaining of having no me time, the sleepless nights, the toys all over, and the constant tidying up, I still wanted another little monkey. I *love* to teach them, be with them, cuddle with them, and play with them. I had always wanted to have a lot of kids, and I dreamed of future family gatherings where all the kids would come home with their own families, grandkids running around and memories being made. I dreamed of our home being HOME for the kids—that loving, fun place that just warms the heart and puts a smile on your face.

During this last pregnancy, I sat with my thoughts for a while. I was so alone; if you are a mom, you probably know what I'm talking about. Your friends who have kids that are not the same age as yours don't come over as much, and the ones who don't have any kids don't come over at all. Everyone is so busy with their own activities. My husband was my rock and he was so supportive, but I just needed a friend to talk to who would understand. Many times, I would hear myself saying "I just want my mom"; she would have been over all the time and offering to help. And then I really wanted to talk to my one brother as well—he would have totally understood me and my upset—but he too had passed about five years prior to my mom.

Thankfully, the Universe was preparing to step in and guide

me. I've always known that I was intuitive in some small way; I feel energy, and I am aware that things show up for a reason. The Universe gives you signs of the direction you should go, but for a long time I just wasn't listening. I kept closing the door on the Divine when she just wanted to help. Now, it was time for me to take notice.

Back when I first met my husband, I was trying to decide what career path to take. My main interest was in nutrition, but I was also interested in other things like makeup. I researched schools and found a private natural nutrition school nearby. I chatted with the school, got their pamphlet, and thought I was going to join, but instead I went down a different path and became a makeup artist. Fast forward to September 2015, nineteen years almost to the same month that I was going to sign up for the natural nutrition program. My kids were six, three, and one, and we were trying for our fourth child. I was going through some old pictures and such, organizing and throwing things out that weren't needed, and didn't I come across THAT pamphlet. I realized that the Universe might be trying to tell me something.

Later that day, I get an email from a site I subscribe to called Crazy Sexy Cancer, which is run by a woman named Kris Carr who reversed her inoperable cancer through nutrition. In the email, Kris raved about this holistic health coaching course from the Institute of Integrative Nutrition. It stuck out like fireworks going off. This is the moment I really became grounded and connected and recognized that the Universe was subtly guiding me in the direction I was meant to go. It was time to listen and to rewrite my story—time to let go of the past, of the old me that I needed to realize didn't exist anymore.

It was time to start my new journey.

My passion has always been to help people, but my new

passion was to help MOMS. I was a mom on a mission, determined to help other to moms not feel the way that I have. Was taking this course the right decision? I wasn't sure, but I needed to trust my intuition and go with it. I needed to feed my brain. I CRAVE knowledge, I really do, especially around how to heal the body both physically and mentally.

The holistic health coaching course was the most amazing course I had ever taken. It opened my eyes; I must have had blinders on before, because now I saw so much more. I completed the course while I was pregnant with my fourth baby, going to the library weekly to do the online modules. It wasn't easy doing this course over the ten months that it ran; with the demands of the kids, the lack of sleep, and the energy required to grow another human being, this momma was exhausted. But, I didn't give up!

I remember doing my final exam in the library and having awful pains in my belly. At first I thought they were just Braxton Hicks contractions as the baby wasn't due until the next week, but I ended up having my fourth baby that night. Thank goodness I did the exam that day! Otherwise, I wouldn't have been able to take the exam, pass it, and become a Holistic Health Coach.

When I started this course, I was at a low. I was lonely and lacking in confidence and self-worth. My thoughts and energy were taken by the kids, who needed me for everything. I was drained inside, but most people couldn't see it. I would joke about it in a truthful way, hoping someone would say, "Hey Nina, would you like some help? Would you like to come out with me and my friends?" When you hear a mom joke around like this, assume it's not a joke and she really does NEED to get out. Ask her out—you will touch her heart in many ways!

At the same time that I started my course, I met a soulful

beauty named Gabby through our homeschooling group who invited me to a weekend intensive feminine movement gathering. I had no clue what this was, but I felt such a pull to go. I messaged the lady in charge asking if there might be one spot available, only to be told no. I prayed, asking the universe to PLEASE make this happen if I was meant to go, and three days later a spot opened up. I was in, but what exactly had I gotten myself into? I had no clue what to expect.

I spent the weekend learning about how many women are disconnected from their feminine—from their true essence. The days were filled with journaling, exploring, listening, music, dance, movement, and soulful pole dance. We were encouraged to let go of our ego and just be within ourselves. We learned to slow down, breathe, and listen to the voice inside as she spoke.

The world can be very busy, but if you take a moment to breathe and just BE, you will see the stillness all around you. I personally am starting to see the calm. I had to go through all this hardship to snap out of being with the "pack of sheep," running through my chaotic daily life thinking there was no time for me, in order to find that peace and strength. I could now see that there was always time, I just had to understand what to do to find that calm.

Through all that had happened, my Feminine Fire had been smothered; it definitely wasn't shining as bright or as strong as it should. I knew my flame was capable of such strength, but after years of spending all of my energy on my kids and family, there was nothing left. I forgot to feed and nurture my inner flame, and I didn't pay attention to any of the signs that it was fading.

The next step in my healing process was yoga. Although I had never done yoga before, I was guided to take the yoga teacher training course and I jumped on it. When the universe speaks, you listen. I signed up when my fourth baby was just a few months old, but I discovered that I wasn't ready so I dropped out. Maybe the universe wanted me to be with a different group, or maybe I just wasn't exactly ready at that time. However, I went back a year later and it was the perfect timing. I was in a different frame of mind, and I was so much stronger than the previous year. I regretted not starting yoga sooner—it felt so good on the body!

By the end of the course, many people were asking if I was going to teach a high intensity style because of my abundance of energy and my background in weight training. But, even though I'm full of fire, I was drawn to the slow movements where I could focus on breathing, go deep within, and find my Feminine Fire—that deep internal flame that makes a woman so beautiful and strong. The slow movement is what my body craved; the same feminine movement I experienced in pole dance. My practice for myself now consists of merging the two together, and my body just soaks it all up.

Healing was taking place without me having to go find help. I no longer accepted that "this is how things are supposed to be"; you know, when you have kids and things just "change." Many women give up on their dreams, passions, and desires once they have children. They were brought up with their Feminine Fire burning so small that they don't know what they are truly capable of. They don't realize how important they are and how much this world needs that woman with a blazing fire inside her.

The next thing the Universe guided me towards was reiki. The funny thing is my mom took a level one reiki course back when I was a young and had an attitude towards anything my parents wanted to show me. I never really listened to her when she spoke of "healing with energy" at that time, but look what

I am into now, twenty years later. If only I had listened back then, man, my Feminine Fire would be *shining*. It would be a huge fireball, like the Sun! But maybe I just wasn't ready for it then. The universe needed me to go through hardship to see and experience how energy works and how healing takes place so that I could help others. So really, my hardship is a gift, and I am so grateful for it.

I signed up for a level one and two reiki course in the spring of 2018, right after I graduated from my yoga course. The connection I felt to this practice was insane. I loved the grounding, the connecting, the mediations, the traveling within meditation, and the meeting of those in the third heavens and above—something that is so hard to even explain. The beauty of reiki is that it can be done both in person and at a distance, which is beneficial for me as my clients are located all over the world. Why didn't I do this sooner? Oh yes, that's right. It wasn't time yet.

I went on to finish my masters in Holy Fire II Karuna Usui Reiki. I took this course with Evelyn King, who opened up her house to teach these courses with her supportive husband, Jim. The other women who took the course and I had an incredible connection and experienced such transformation. I am forever grateful for Evelyn teaching and guiding us on how to heal, connect, and get grounded.

Next on my journey was courses on tapping, which came the summer of 2018. Tapping, known as EFT, is all about releasing stuck emotions from the past. We carry our emotions in the cells of our body for years and years, and those past emotions come up and affect our daily lives. Releasing them and letting go makes a huge impact on the body as stuck emotions can create illness and dis-ease.

Once you mix these all together—Holy Fire II reiki, yoga,

feminine movement, EFT, being a fitness expert, and the holistic health and life coaching on top of it all—and you have something truly amazing.

Now, just because I've taken all these courses, have really gotten connected and grounded, and have finally found my path again doesn't mean that everything is easy breezy. It's still work. Like any other relationship or career, just because things are going great doesn't mean you stop trying. You have to put in the time to nurture yourself every day, and when you slip off of this path you need to know how to reconnect and get grounded.

I still have the chaos around me; the kids still always need me for something. I homeschool my six- and nine-year-olds. My four-year-old wants to join in, so I give him fun letters and numbers to do while my two-year-old plays around us. Oh wait, I didn't mention that I also homeschool them? This is why I *need* and crave time for myself, although my cravings are for business, sports, and helping others, not the spa. My choice to homeschool wasn't because I thought I would be a better teacher, or that I wanted an Einstein. My goal is to teach them LIFE, and to teach them what I've learned so far. I want to show them how to live with passion and how to connect, be connected, and reconnect when they slip off. And I want you to learn these lessons as well.

I really wanted to share not only my story but also an outline to follow so you can get yourself on a journey back to YOU; to feel, to connect, and to be the woman you are meant to be. And it starts TODAY. We have one life on this earth, and there is no rewind and no pause button. It just keeps going.

Don't go through life with empty dreams, lost passion, and no self-worth. To start feeling better today and making a difference in your life, try changing your morning routine. I recommend starting with meditation when you first wake, just lying there and taking the time to breathe. Imagine negative energy being released with each exhale and positive energy and love coming in with each inhale. When you are coming to the end of that light mediation, finish it off with some affirmations that are needed for YOU as well as some appreciation and gratitude for you, this life, and all you have. Some of my personal affirmations are "I am love," "I am loved," "Abundance flows to me with ease and grace," "I am powerful and strong," "I am a great coach," and "I am a GREAT mom." The Universe listens to all of your thoughts. It doesn't know the difference between negative and positive, it just responds to what it hears. So, when you say something like "I don't want to be broke," the Universe just hears "want" and "broke." Instead, say what you WANT—or, better yet, say it like you have it already.

As you get yourself ready for the day, have a glass of freshly squeezed lemon in warm water and read a chapter or two out of a great inspiring, motivational, or self-help book, or take this time to journal whatever comes to mind. Once you are done with this step, plan your day. It's tough to stick to a structured schedule at times, especially with kids underfoot, so just jot down what you'd like to accomplish and go with the flow.

Put on some relaxing music and slowly move your body through yoga poses, dancing, or whatever feels right to you. Keep your breath slow like you did in your morning meditation and just be with yourself. Listen to your soul. It is amazing how good you will feel just from this short little practice. Take time during the day to just sit and be present with whatever is going on around you. Be still for just a few minutes and send gratitude out to the universe. "Thank you, thank you, thank you."

If you're not sure if you will have time to incorporate these practices into your morning schedule, then wake up just a little earlier than normal so you have time to give some love to your soul. Starting a new, healthy pattern will help you manifest your goals and dreams and help you create a life and body you deserve. Listen to your intuition—that's the Universe whispering to you, directing you to where you are supposed to go. We all have this power, and the more you do some of these practices the more in tune you will be.

Your Feminine Fire is ready to burn as big and bright as you want it to. It is there to create passion, confidence, awareness, and creativity, and to express so much love. Every single woman has it, but if you can't find it don't feel helpless or lost. Instead, try one of the approaches I've mentioned to help get things started. It's these small steps, daily or weekly, that will get you to that powerful, beautiful soul you have inside you. The chaos and the negativity will always come and go; it's how long we let it sit and how we choose to deal with it that counts.

I will leave you with my favorite quote that I have on my wall so that my family and I can ready it daily, several times a day in fact, and be reminded of our greatness, even amongst the chaos. Read this, and be reminded.

"Our deepest fear is not that we are inadequate. Our deepest fear is that we are powerful beyond measure. It is our light, not our darkness that most frightens us. We ask ourselves, 'Who am I to be brilliant, gorgeous, talented, fabulous?' Actually, who are you not to be? You are a child of God. Your playing small does not serve the world. There is nothing enlightened about shrinking so that other people won't feel insecure around you. We are all meant to shine, as children do. We were born to make manifest the glory of God that is within us. It's not just in some of us; it's in everyone. And as we let our own light shine, we unconsciously give other people permission to do the same. As we are liberated from our own fear, our presence automatically liberates others."

—Marianne Williamson, A Return to Love

About Nina Luchka

Nina is passionate about helping moms create a life and body they love and reconnect to their inner Feminine Fire. Through her own struggles and challenges that came from being a mom of four and an entrepreneur, she gained a wealth of knowledge in fitness, nutrition, energy healing, wellness, and self-care.

Nina has stepped on the best stages in the world as an IFBB pro, including the Arnold Schwarzenegger Class, competing against the best in the world. She is a fitness expert, Professional IFBB Figure Athlete, Holy Fire II Karuna Usui Reiki Master, EFT Level 2 Practitioner, Conditioning Coach, Feminine Fire Coach, Yoga Teacher, Holistic Health Coach, and nature lover. She also homeschools her kids, Aspen (nine), Cruz (six), Knox (four), and Steihl (two).

Nina guides women to find their passion and sparking their inner Feminine Fire through exercise, feminine movement, life coaching, nutrition, holistic wellness, and energy work. To find out more, please contact her at one of the links below.

www.ninaluchka.com
Facebook: Nina Luchka
Instagram: @ninaluchka

10

From Whispers to Wonder Woman

by Stephanie Roman

Chapter 10

From Whispers to Wonder Woman

If you asked me when the first time was that I heard the voice, I wouldn't know the answer—it's been with me for as long as I can remember. As I was growing up extremely poor in the seedy areas of town, the voice would usually appear after a particularly bad beating from the abuser I was living with, urging me to "keep going, don't give up!" The ironic thing is that many of the beatings I received when I was younger centered around not "feeling the spirit" in church. Even though I knew the punishment would be severe, I never once faked having a "God experience." It was a sacred experience that I wanted to have more than anything in the world and yet felt like I never did. The loneliness of feeling not worthy of such a relationship often left me sobbing on my bed, wondering what made me so utterly unlovable that God wouldn't even speak to me.

I was always taught, not only by my birth mother and step-father but by all of society, that appearance mattered more than anything else in the world. I had an image that I swore I would uphold: the image of Barbie. When I received a Barbie at age three, I cried tears of true joy for the first time as I looked at the ideal image of an "American beauty." This perfect feminine ideal became everything I strove for in life, and as a type A perfectionist this goal soon became an obsession. By the age of seventeen I was waking up early to flat iron my bleached-blonde hair and carrying my flat iron with me to repeat the process in bathrooms throughout the day. I made sure that my weight was what I saw as "Barbie trim," but when I look at pictures of myself from this time I can see that I was actually emaciated and borderline anorexic.

My dream of finding my Ken—an all American,

blonde-haired, blue-eyed tennis all-star from a well-off family—became a reality when I was a freshman in college. I fell hard. This man was witty, charming, and smart, and he was physically all that I had ever imagined. We dated for ten years before getting married and moving to a prestigious part of Dallas not that far from George W. Bush.

Inside my Barbie dream house, though, life was not so picturesque. I had unknowingly recreated my childhood with this man. Abuse became a daily occurrence, and at the age of twenty-six I was so beaten down that my body began to rebel. At the time it seemed like my health began failing "all of a sudden," but the reality was that it was the cumulation of over two decades of internalizing stress and abuse, trying to make people love me who were definitely not conducive to a healthy life. I began to get sick from almost every food I ate, and a parade of fancy, high-priced specialists became a cornerstone of my existence. Test were run, dietary restrictions were imposed, and prescriptions were written. It took over three years to reach the final diagnosis of Crohn's disease—the very first of the six autoimmune diseases I've been diagnosed with as of today. The war with my body had begun, and that's when I remember hearing the voice more clearly than I had in years; it had become repressed due to my practice of numbing myself with antidepressants, anti-anxiety medicine, drugs, and alcohol.

I remember being laid out in my bathroom, sobbing against the toilet and begging the God that I thought wanted nothing to do with me to make the stomach cramps stop. I said, "I can't do this anymore, please take me home." Suddenly, my thoughts were filled with the voice, saying, "KEEP GOING. KEEP GOING. KEEP GOING." It didn't sound like God, it sounded just like me. At the moment, I couldn't figure out why I would tell myself such a thing when all I wanted to do was die.

I was put on steroids and my already tiny frame continued to wither down to almost nothing. Today I weigh 138 pounds, and I look healthy. I weighed 79 pounds on my wedding day. Nothing was ever enough for my husband, though; he would make comments about how I didn't look like I did when I was nineteen, or that he couldn't understand how I could be happy with my body.

Nothing was ever enough for my work either. I was a marketing coordinator for a private real estate firm and I worked almost non-stop. I was in charge of coordinating and planning all of the broker events for the company across eight states, including ours. One of the strongly implied parts of the job was that I was to look a certain way in order to be presentable to brokers, even though the stress of maintaining this image on top of the overload of working hours was nearly impossible. The more I tried to please everyone, the worse my health became and the more the external forces in my life required more from me.

At twenty-seven I had a "slight" cardiac arrest and was rushed to the hospital despite my pleas to stay at home; I just wanted to die, and having it happen through natural causes seemed better than outright attempting suicide. When I arrived at the hospital, I wasn't receiving proper oxygen and my lips and fingernails had turned blue. Then, my skin started to break out in huge weeping sores and rashes. A fleet of dermatologists tried in vain to solve my skin issues, and again another autoimmune disease was uncovered. Once I was stable, I was sent back home.

The voice came back after a particularly hard day of abuse that found me crumpled in a heap on the floor in my Barbie dream house bathroom, once again begging to be taken home. "KEEP GOING!" it shouted, and I could only cry in response.

Age twenty-eight brought a six-and-a-half-minute seizure and another trip to the hospital. The doctors said it was a miracle I was alive and hadn't suffered any brain damage. I kept wondering why I was being forced to endure living in this body when it was literally dying. I was having full blown panic attacks by this point, and the doctor's solution was to pump me full of antidepressants and three heavy duty anti-anxiety medications, which dulled the voice I was hearing to a murmur. I was grateful to not have to hear what I believed at that time to be a punishment—a voice that I could never satisfy and always dragged me through the hardest times of my life.

I have always wanted to be a mother and I have a great connection with children, so much so that for years I was a nanny for many families of twins and triplets. My husband and I started to try for children shortly before we got married, and three-and-a-half months before our wedding day I found out we had successfully conceived. I anxiously awaited the ultrasound to confirm the pregnancy and was so incredibly happy to see that the embryos had taken—yes, we were having twins! Now that the waiting period was over, I joyously told friends and family the good news.

The day before our wedding, I started bleeding heavily and experiencing intense cramps. I drove myself to the OBGYN, and after having an ultrasound I was given the news that both babies were dead, and I would have to take pills to discard the rest of the tissue. My body was too beaten down to carry the pregnancy to term. It felt as though the world had come crashing down around me, but I was too tired to be mad. I still held my outer appearance together because it was all I knew how to do. I walked down the aisle in Depends, bleeding out the two lives that I was sure I would give birth to. The voice was dull, but still there. "Keep going, keep going, keep going."

Over the next two years, I would go on to have eleven miscarriages.

I was able to hide my ailments not only from not my employer, but most of my family and friends as well—up until my twenty-eighth birthday, that is, when my once extremely thick hair began to fall out by the handful. I remember waking up a couple of times and thinking that I was drowning because so much hair had fallen in and around my mouth and nose while I slept. I started wearing wigs to hide the loss from everyone around me, still determined that I wouldn't let my image slip. Soon, I received my diagnosis of alopecia universalis. It was the least life-threatening out of all of my autoimmune diseases, and yet it was the one that destroyed my life the most.

The wigs I wore were uncomfortable, but I put up with them for as long as I could because it was expected that I would wear them. This discomfort came to a head when I was at my grandparents' church one summer day. The air conditioner wasn't working and the sweltering Texas heat was palpable to everyone, much less someone in a very hot, very itchy wig. I snuck off to the bathroom and desperately tried to put wet paper towels under my wig to cool myself down, but nothing was working other than removing it completely. I was pissed at the situation, REALLY pissed, and all the "why me's" and the never-ending pity party that I was hosting became even louder. Then, I heard the voice say, "You are stronger than this. Are you really going to let baldness stop you after all you've been through? Keep going, but without the wig." And for once, I followed the voice's advice. I defiantly put the wig in my purse, scrubbed the makeup off of my face, and marched out into the sanctuary. Now, doing this would have been terrifying enough as is, but everyone in my grandparents' small church had known me literally from birth. NONE of them knew I had any hair loss, much less that I was completely bald without even eyebrows or eyelashes. I can't even imagine the bewilderment and surprise they must have felt as they saw me return from the bathroom with no makeup and no wig. I did see the looks of surprise and awe, but I clung to the voice that was now cheering me on and ignored them.

From that moment on, I never wore a wig again. This was not at ALL what my husband or my bosses wanted, and man did I ever hear about it. Despite persuasion and punishment, I held my ground.

My husband filed for divorce shortly after our two-year wedding anniversary—I wasn't Barbie, so I wasn't of use anymore and I was discarded. I was also let go from my job shortly before the divorce, and all my friends except one chose to side with my husband. I now was twenty-nine, bald, alone, and unemployed. This turn of events blindsided me, and I kept wondering why the voice had led me down this path. I felt as if I was dying, completely terrified and not wanting to survive. More devastation and loss came when a routine gyno visit brought news of infertility. A big part of me felt like it died on that day, and yet still I kept going, unsure of why or how or what the voice wanted me to do, and even more uncertain of whether I could actually do it.

My safe haven in times of doubt or uncertainty has always been helping others. In fact, when I was asked what I wanted to be when I grew up, I would respond, "I just want to help people." Most times this was followed by questions about HOW I wanted to help people, and honestly I had no idea. I also thought it was in the stars for me to have children and that raising them would be one way that I helped people, but those dreams were squashed. In my darkest moment I decided to volunteer at a children's oncology ward, and as is often the case, these children were the ones who helped me instead of the other way around. Faced with the pain and uncertainty of such a cruel disease as cancer, these bald little heroes soldiered on without a complaint and with a smile on their faces. The scene was set for my life-changing epiphany.

One cold winter's day, I was visiting with one of my favorite children, a little three-year-old girl. She was chattering happily away to me as she received her chemotherapy treatment when a woman appeared carrying a package that I knew very well. The little girl unwrapped a Barbie doll and began to sob with joy, but this Barbie was different than the one I had received at that very age—this Barbie was bald. In that instant, all of my previous tragedies became a blessing, a gift, instead of the death sentence I previously saw them as. The voice was back: "THIS is why you keep going." In that moment, I saw a vision of my mission on this Earth. I was to remind women of their own unique beauty, and to use my platform of baldness to do so.

With the help of my life coach, Emily Rose, I launched The Bald Barbie Army, a passion project that vowed to redefine beauty one doll at a time. I enlisted in Toastmasters—a public speaking organization—and as a result, word of my venture spread like wildfire. I began speaking at Kiwanis clubs, the Boys and Girls Club of America, and private corporate venues. The voice was louder than ever. Even after ditching my anxiety medications, knowing that I could do without them and in fact *needed* to do so in order to live my fullest life, I had the strong urge to follow through with opportunities that once would have left me in the fetal position just by hearing about them. Each time I acted on what the voice told me to do or pursued an experience that took me FAR outside my comfort zone, I had tremendous success.

I also began to take better care of myself. I changed the food I ate, I began to meditate every day, and I journaled. Instead of frantically trying to make others happy or seeking answers for what would make me happy from an external source, I found the courage to listen only to that guiding voice. At first, reorienting myself to hear this voice and take the action steps to lead a healthy lifestyle was a process. As women, we are so distracted by the outside world and have been so conditioned to take care of others all the time that we don't prioritize ourselves. However, each time I listened to myself and succeeded, I became even more resolute in the decisions I made. I began to trust myself for the first time in my whole life, and with this trust and confidence, my perspective continued to change. I stayed positive—not in a way where I feared thinking anything negative or ran from having a bad day, but from the vantage point of seeing the best in myself and others. I understood that I had outgrown a lot of people from my past, and I started telling myself every day that my badass tribe of ladies was on its way. I held on to this vibration until seemingly all at once, women began to appear. How badass are these women? Well, you only have to read any of these chapters to see for yourself. Wonder Women like these are my new normal. The girl who could never remember having a group of people who truly cared for her was engulfed in ladies who genuinely saw and loved me for who I am and were on the same Earth healing, light, and love path as I was. The voice continued to make more and more sense.

I "came out" as a psychic on Facebook live two years ago. Not a soul knew I had these abilities outside of my mom and dad, my boyfriend at the time, the few people I had read for to test my abilities, and my life coach. The anticipated reality of telling the world that I was psychic was beyond scary. I lived in Dallas and thought that I would be shunned by the largely religious community. However, the voice was still there, and I knew by this point to listen to it. I knew that this voice was loving and would lead me to my own happiness more accurately than anyone else ever had.

When I made the announcement, I wasn't seen as the sideshow, the freak, or the weirdo that I was so terrified of being seen as. People were curious, of course, but as I became more confident in my abilities, I started to realize that most people had their own story about hearing a voice. Sometimes the voice was dull and quiet like mine had once been, and most of the time people told me that they heard it in their own voice. My psychic business, Divine Intervention Readings, began to shift from providing "one-off" readings to teaching people— primarily women—how they could embrace their own gifts.

I believe that everyone is born psychic, but we all have different abilities and ways that the messages come through. When I was searching for ways to embrace my abilities, I found that most of the literature out there only highlighted one of the ways you get messages. I found it EXTREMELY frustrating to essentially be back in the place of trying to make my unique abilities fit into a predetermined box, much like the Barbie box that I never fit into despite my best efforts. The more I tried to just be one thing, to just receive messages in one way, the less I felt psychic at all and the harder it was to hear the voice.

One day, it dawned on me that each of us has our own "psychic fingerprint." The analogy I use with my clients is to picture that every psychic ability is a crayon. The courses and books I found were trying to have you grab ONE crayon and color with it. In contrast, my abilities were like dumping out a box of 100 crayons and coloring with all of them at once. As soon as I had this epiphany, the voice was louder than ever. "KEEP GOING!" Instead of questioning every little step of how and what I was supposed to do, I started to relax and believe that I would know when I was supposed to know. Every time I relaxed, I would hear or feel another step to take.

I realized that this was another one of my purposes in life. I wanted to help women who were in a similar place as I had been—ones that had tried all of the "shoulds" placed on us by society and had realized that these alone weren't enough to get the job done. Women began appearing in my life that reminded me of me back when I was lost. They were overworked, overwhelmed, and depleted. They swore they couldn't be psychic, and the voice gave me clear instructions to remind them of who they really are. I started a program titled "An Apprenticeship to Divinity" and began to have one-on-one sessions with these women to channel for them and give them customized meditations and exercises that would allow them to hear their own voice more clearly. The results even astonished me. Every single one of these women now KNOW they are psychic. They remember their power and their connection with the Divine and with all living things. They have a clear sense of purpose and understand that they are not alone. The most incredible result is that these women know how to make their own happily ever after, and they are doing it. They no longer allow the world to deplete and defeat them. Yes, they are still caregivers, but they do so from a place of taking care of themselves FIRST and everyone else second. The more that I see these results, the more I understand my place in this world.

Shortly after I created my apprenticeship program, I received news that after eight rounds of auditioning, I had landed a Tedx talk. The Bald Barbie Army mission was shared with a large audience at Mountain View College in Dallas, Texas. It was a dream come true and provided even more validation to me that I was on the right track in both of my businesses.

The road wasn't just paved with amazing opportunities though. Last summer, I initiated a break up with my boyfriend of almost two years because I knew we weren't right for each other; it was the first time I had ever put my own feelings first in a romantic relationship. Shortly afterwards, my Grandma, who had always been more like a mother to me, passed away. At this same time, I was also being affected by a crazy planetary influence that left me with so much stored up energy that it was as if I was drinking non-stop espresso, even though I don't drink any caffeine at all. I began to slide back into negative self-talk, a pattern that was perpetuated by years of verbal abuse. I had kicked this a couple of years before, but now it was coming back with a vengeance. My friends all told me I wasn't going backwards, even though I felt like I was, and that the right time for the next move in my career and personal life would come. As I sought my next step, I signed up for an intensive twelve-week class with my new thought church that taught the foundations of what our faith is about as well as ways to apply it to everyday life, and I dove into being on the praise and worship band. The months went by achingly slow.

One day, I was at one of my best friend's house for an eat and pray—an event where she makes fabulous food and we pray on whatever is bothering us at that time—when I began to open up about my frustration of not knowing how to keep going even though this is what I taught others. I remember crying to her, "I know I'm supposed to get my message out to more people at once, but I have no idea how I'll do that." Right then and there, she prayed for me that I would be shown the next step.

This chapter is my next step—the door that I was impatiently searching for but couldn't seem to find—and you, dear reader, are the answer to my prayers. In my church class, they reminded us that all we have to do to find our next step is to ask ourselves what we really want. It sounds simplistic, but I've found that a lot of times I focus on what I DON'T want. I'm also a very active overanlayzer and overthinker, so I'll plan out how to do something without actually examining what I want to get out of it. When I asked myself what I really wanted shortly before being approached by the angelic Bev Adamo to write this chapter, the answer was simple: I want to help women who feel alone, isolated, unhappy, helpless, and hopeless, and are searching for their door. From the bottom of my heart, I want to remind you of who you really are. This something I emphasize with all of my clients: I'm not teaching you anything that you don't already know, I am simply here to REMIND you of what you knew when you came into this world that society has conditioned you to forget. You have allowed the world to take its toll on you for way too long. I want to remind you of the power you have that is just waiting for you to remember and to step back into it. You are perfect in this moment. You are the reason I exist, and I won't stop until I'm able to tell all of you to stop running and listen to your voice.

The voice I've told you about isn't a gift that I have and you don't. It's not a relationship you have to earn or that you are unworthy of, regardless of anything you have ever done. This voice is God, and it's in you just as strongly as it's in me. It's waiting for you to claim it as your own, but no one can do this for you. You must make a decision to find YOUR happiness and cling desperately to that decision no matter what. I'm not saying you can't have bad days—days when you are tired of the voice that's seemingly leading you down a path that isn't where you want to go. I'm saying that once you commit to being the best version of yourself, the version that you most likely don't see in you right now, the world will begin to change. You will transform into your own Wonder Woman, even if the process is slower than you would like. You will call to you like-minded, supportive people that will help you travel this path. Everything you have ever wanted is waiting for you once you remember your beautiful, perfect, unique power.

You, dear one, are a perfect gift that deserves to be happy and healthy. You are a miracle, just as everything in this world is, but you will never see it if you don't take the leap of faith to do something scary—like writing this chapter. I'm terrified of what I'm doing, and that's how I know that doing it is worthwhile. I have a saying, "push past the place of puke," which basically means to go outside of your comfort zone over and over and over. I feel the energy of events that haven't happened yet in my body. People feel this in many different ways, but to me it's the feeling of dry heaving. For the majority of my life, this feeling terrified me enough that I continued to shrink back within my comfort zone and play small. When I realized that if I pushed through the feeling I would have the most magical, amazing experiences, I began to dry heave a lot. And every time, this feeling has been worth it.

As much as I'd like to say that I can make the decision for you to move forward undauntingly into your great unknown with the commitment to following your instincts, your God voice, and your happy, I can't. YOU are in charge of changing your life, of finding you again, and of finding your place in this world.

You've lived so long in the comfortable but stationary. Now, it's time to dust your cape off, grab the hands of your sisters, and begin your power path.

About Stephanie Roman

Stephanie was born and raised in Dallas, Texas, where she still lives today. She accredits her personal and spiritual growth over the last five years to her tremendously supportive family, especially her father and mother Scott and Ida Noack, her amazing friends, and her life coach Emily Rose. Without these people she wouldn't be stretched past her comfort zone over and over again. Her mentor, Bev Adamo, continuously brings magic and wonder into Stephanie's life, including the opportunity to write her story in this book.

Stephanie is a Tedx motivational speaker and advocate for girls' and women's unique beauty with her passion project, The Bald Barbie Army. She loves to inspire and empower women to live life to the fullest and be proud in their own skin.

Stephanie is also a proud psychic. Her company, Divine Intervention Readings, teaches people that everyone is psychic in their own ways. She educates people on how to access their inner psychic through programs that allow people to explore and remember their own "psychic fingerprint" of their abilities. Divine Intervention Readings can be found on its Facebook business page.

Facebook: Divine Intervention Readings